MW01701402

Microsoft SharePoint Serv
Complete Self-Assessment Guide

The guidance in this Self-Assessment is based on Microsoft SharePoint Server best practices and standards in business process architecture, design and quality management. The guidance is also based on the professional judgment of the individual collaborators listed in the Acknowledgments.

Table of Contents

About The Art of Service

The Art of Service, Business Process Architects since 2000, is dedicated to helping stakeholders achieve excellence.

Defining, designing, creating, and implementing a process to solve a stakeholders challenge or meet an objective is the most valuable role... In EVERY group, company, organization and department.

Unless you're talking a one-time, single-use project, there should be a process. Whether that process is managed and implemented by humans, AI, or a combination of the two, it needs to be designed by someone with a complex enough perspective to ask the right questions.

Someone capable of asking the right questions and step back and say, 'What are we really trying to accomplish here? And is there a different way to look at it?'

With The Art of Service's Standard Requirements Self-Assessments, we empower people who can do just that — whether their title is marketer, entrepreneur, manager, salesperson, consultant, Business Process Manager, executive assistant, IT Manager, CIO etc... —they are the people who rule the future. They are people who watch the process as it happens, and ask the right questions to make the process work better.

Contact us when you need any support with this Self-Assessment and any help with templates, blue-prints and examples of standard documents you might need:

http://theartofservice.com
service@theartofservice.com

Acknowledgments

This checklist was developed under the auspices of The Art of Service, chaired by Gerardus Blokdyk.

Representatives from several client companies participated in the preparation of this Self-Assessment.

In addition, we are thankful for the design and printing services provided.

Included Resources - how to access

Included with your purchase of the book is the Microsoft SharePoint Server Self-Assessment Spreadsheet Dashboard which contains all questions and Self-Assessment areas and auto-generates insights, graphs, and project RACI planning - all with examples to get you started right away.

How? Simply send an email to
access@theartofservice.com
with this books' title in the subject to get the Microsoft SharePoint Server Self Assessment Tool right away.

You will receive the following contents with New and Updated specific criteria:

- The latest quick edition of the book in PDF
- The latest complete edition of the book in PDF, which criteria correspond to the criteria in...
- The Self-Assessment Excel Dashboard, and...
- Example pre-filled Self-Assessment Excel Dashboard to get familiar with results generation
- In-depth specific Checklists covering the topic
- Project management checklists and templates to assist with implementation

INCLUDES LIFETIME SELF ASSESSMENT UPDATES

Every self assessment comes with Lifetime Updates and Lifetime Free Updated Books. Lifetime Updates is an industry-first feature which allows you to receive verified self assessment updates, ensuring you always have the most accurate information at your fingertips.

Get it now- you will be glad you did - do it now, before you forget.

Send an email to **access@theartofservice.com** with this books' title in the subject to get the Microsoft SharePoint Server Self Assessment Tool right away.

Your feedback is invaluable to us

If you recently bought this book, we would love to hear from you! You can do this by writing a review on amazon (or the online store where you purchased this book) about your last purchase! As part of our continual service improvement process, we love to hear real client experiences and feedback.

How does it work?
To post a review on Amazon, just log in to your account and click on the Create Your Own Review button (under Customer Reviews) of the relevant product page. You can find examples of product reviews in Amazon. If you purchased from another online store, simply follow their procedures.

What happens when I submit my review?
Once you have submitted your review, send us an email at review@theartofservice.com with the link to your review so we can properly thank you for your feedback.

Purpose of this Self-Assessment

This Self-Assessment has been developed to improve understanding of the requirements and elements of Microsoft SharePoint Server, based on best practices and standards in business process architecture, design and quality management.

It is designed to allow for a rapid Self-Assessment to determine how closely existing management practices and procedures correspond to the elements of the Self-Assessment.

The criteria of requirements and elements of Microsoft SharePoint Server have been rephrased in the format of a Self-Assessment questionnaire, with a seven-criterion scoring system, as explained in this document.

In this format, even with limited background knowledge of

Microsoft SharePoint Server, a manager can quickly review existing operations to determine how they measure up to the standards. This in turn can serve as the starting point of a 'gap analysis' to identify management tools or system elements that might usefully be implemented in the organization to help improve overall performance.

How to use the Self-Assessment

On the following pages are a series of questions to identify to what extent your Microsoft SharePoint Server initiative is complete in comparison to the requirements set in standards.

To facilitate answering the questions, there is a space in front of each question to enter a score on a scale of '1' to '5'.

1 Strongly Disagree

2 Disagree

3 Neutral

4 Agree

5 Strongly Agree

Read the question and rate it with the following in front of mind:

**'In my belief,
the answer to this question is clearly defined'.**

There are two ways in which you can choose to interpret this statement;

1. how aware are you that the answer to the question is clearly defined
2. for more in-depth analysis you can choose to gather

evidence and confirm the answer to the question. This obviously will take more time, most Self-Assessment users opt for the first way to interpret the question and dig deeper later on based on the outcome of the overall Self-Assessment.

A score of '1' would mean that the answer is not clear at all, where a '5' would mean the answer is crystal clear and defined. Leave emtpy when the question is not applicable or you don't want to answer it, you can skip it without affecting your score. Write your score in the space provided.

After you have responded to all the appropriate statements in each section, compute your average score for that section, using the formula provided, and round to the nearest tenth. Then transfer to the corresponding spoke in the Microsoft SharePoint Server Scorecard on the second next page of the Self-Assessment.

Your completed Microsoft SharePoint Server Scorecard will give you a clear presentation of which Microsoft SharePoint Server areas need attention.

Microsoft SharePoint Server Scorecard Example

Example of how the finalized Scorecard can look like:

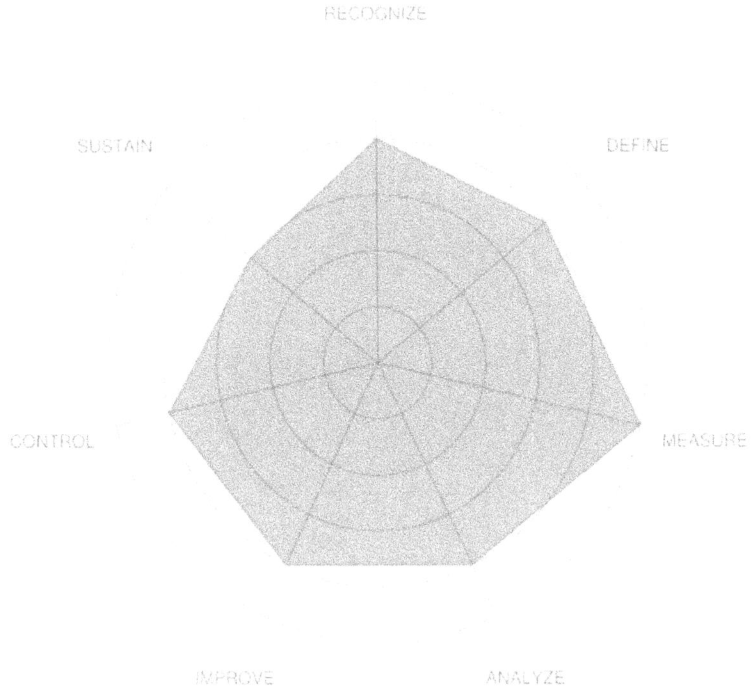

Microsoft SharePoint Server Scorecard

Your Scores:

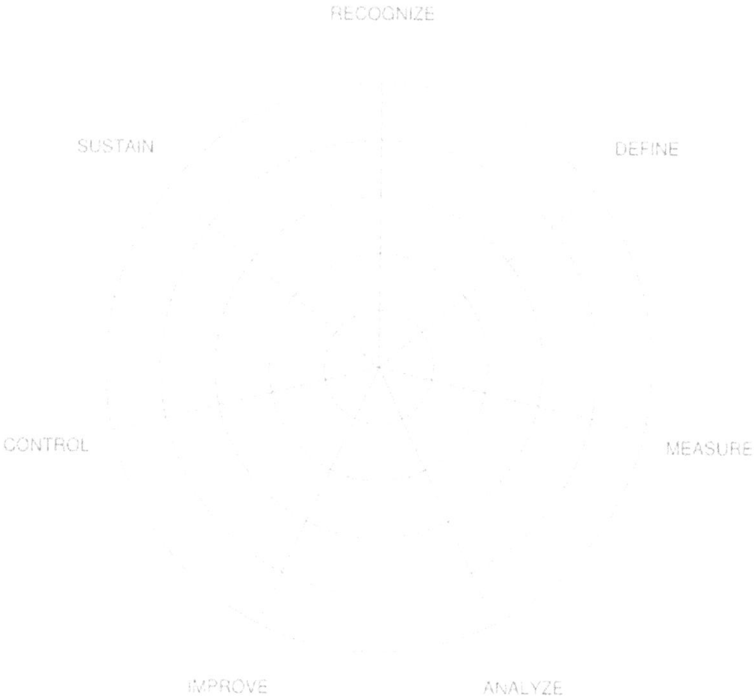

BEGINNING OF THE SELF-ASSESSMENT:

CRITERION #1: RECOGNIZE

INTENT: Be aware of the need for change. Recognize that there is an unfavorable variation, problem or symptom.

In my belief, the answer to this question is clearly defined:

5 Strongly Agree

4 Agree

3 Neutral

2 Disagree

1 Strongly Disagree

1. What problems are you facing and how do you consider Microsoft SharePoint Server will circumvent those obstacles?
<--- Score

2. What are the business objectives to be achieved with Microsoft SharePoint Server?
<--- Score

3. Are problem definition and motivation clearly presented?
<--- Score

4. Who else hopes to benefit from it?
<--- Score

5. How do you identify the kinds of information that you will need?
<--- Score

6. How do you take a forward-looking perspective in identifying Microsoft SharePoint Server research related to market response and models?
<--- Score

7. How much are sponsors, customers, partners, stakeholders involved in Microsoft SharePoint Server? In other words, what are the risks, if Microsoft SharePoint Server does not deliver successfully?
<--- Score

8. What are the expected benefits of Microsoft SharePoint Server to the business?
<--- Score

9. Are there recognized Microsoft SharePoint Server problems?
<--- Score

10. Who needs what information?
<--- Score

11. Can your application prevent concurrent logins?
<--- Score

12. Will a response program recognize when a crisis occurs and provide some level of response?
<--- Score

13. Will it solve real problems?
<--- Score

14. Do you need to retain the functionality?
<--- Score

15. What would happen if Microsoft SharePoint Server weren't done?
<--- Score

16. Do you need different information or graphics?
<--- Score

17. Can management personnel recognize the monetary benefit of Microsoft SharePoint Server?
<--- Score

18. How are you going to measure success?
<--- Score

19. Will Microsoft SharePoint Server deliverables need to be tested and, if so, by whom?
<--- Score

20. Think about the people you identified for your Microsoft SharePoint Server project and the project responsibilities you would assign to them. what kind of training do you think they would need to perform these responsibilities effectively?
<--- Score

21. Are your goals realistic? Do you need to redefine your problem? Perhaps the problem has changed or maybe you have reached your goal and need to set a new one?
<--- Score

22. What do you need to start doing?
<--- Score

23. Are employees recognized or rewarded for performance that demonstrates the highest levels of integrity?
<--- Score

24. For your Microsoft SharePoint Server project, identify and describe the business environment, is there more than one layer to the business environment?
<--- Score

25. Should you invest in industry-recognized qualications?
<--- Score

26. What extra resources will you need?
<--- Score

27. Will new equipment/products be required to facilitate Microsoft SharePoint Server delivery, for example is new software needed?
<--- Score

28. Is it clear when you think of the day ahead of you what activities and tasks you need to complete?
<--- Score

29. What vendors make products that address the Microsoft SharePoint Server needs?
<--- Score

30. To what extent would your organization benefit from being recognized as a award recipient?
<--- Score

31. Consider your own Microsoft SharePoint Server project, what types of organizational problems do you think might be causing or affecting your problem, based on the work done so far?
<--- Score

32. Are there any specific expectations or concerns about the Microsoft SharePoint Server team, Microsoft SharePoint Server itself?
<--- Score

33. How does it fit into your organizational needs and tasks?
<--- Score

34. What are your needs in relation to Microsoft SharePoint Server skills, labor, equipment, and markets?
<--- Score

35. What is the problem or issue?
<--- Score

36. What does Microsoft SharePoint Server success mean to the stakeholders?
<--- Score

37. Is the need for organizational change recognized?

<--- Score

38. What should be considered when identifying available resources, constraints, and deadlines?
<--- Score

39. What are the timeframes required to resolve each of the issues/problems?
<--- Score

40. Are there attachments that need to be incorporated as part of the whole record?
<--- Score

41. How do you assess your Microsoft SharePoint Server workforce capability and capacity needs, including skills, competencies, and staffing levels?
<--- Score

42. What is the smallest subset of the problem you can usefully solve?
<--- Score

43. Are you dealing with any of the same issues today as yesterday? What can you do about this?
<--- Score

44. Do you need to avoid or amend any Microsoft SharePoint Server activities?
<--- Score

45. Are controls defined to recognize and contain problems?
<--- Score

46. Who needs to know about Microsoft SharePoint

Server?
<--- Score

47. What needs to be done?
<--- Score

48. Does your organization need more Microsoft SharePoint Server education?
<--- Score

49. Do you really need all of that information?
<--- Score

50. Do you know what you need to know about Microsoft SharePoint Server?
<--- Score

51. Are there any revenue recognition issues?
<--- Score

52. What training and capacity building actions are needed to implement proposed reforms?
<--- Score

53. What tools and technologies are needed for a custom Microsoft SharePoint Server project?
<--- Score

54. To what extent does each concerned units management team recognize Microsoft SharePoint Server as an effective investment?
<--- Score

55. What else needs to be measured?
<--- Score

56. How are the Microsoft SharePoint Server's objectives aligned to the organization's overall business strategy?
<--- Score

57. Do you have/need 24-hour access to key personnel?
<--- Score

58. What information do users need?
<--- Score

59. Have all project stakeholders been identified?
<--- Score

60. Does Microsoft SharePoint Server create potential expectations in other areas that need to be recognized and considered?
<--- Score

61. What situation(s) led to this Microsoft SharePoint Server Self Assessment?
<--- Score

62. What are the minority interests and what amount of minority interests can be recognized?
<--- Score

63. As a sponsor, customer or management, how important is it to meet goals, objectives?
<--- Score

64. Looking at each person individually – does every one have the qualities which are needed to work in this group?
<--- Score

65. What prevents you from making the changes you know will make you a more effective Microsoft SharePoint Server leader?
<--- Score

66. How can auditing be a preventative security measure?
<--- Score

67. Who had the original idea?
<--- Score

68. When a Microsoft SharePoint Server manager recognizes a problem, what options are available?
<--- Score

69. Are there Microsoft SharePoint Server problems defined?
<--- Score

70. What business need are you addressing?
<--- Score

71. Who defines the rules in relation to any given issue?
<--- Score

72. Are all the interfaces identified?
<--- Score

73. Who are your key stakeholders who need to sign off?
<--- Score

Add up total points for this section:

_____ = Total points for this section

Divided by: ______ (number of statements answered) = ______ Average score for this section

Transfer your score to the Microsoft SharePoint Server Index at the beginning of the Self-Assessment.

CRITERION #2: DEFINE:

INTENT: Formulate the business problem. Define the problem, needs and objectives.

In my belief, the answer to this question is clearly defined:

5 Strongly Agree

4 Agree

3 Neutral

2 Disagree

1 Strongly Disagree

1. What are the boundaries of the scope? What is in bounds and what is not? What is the start point? What is the stop point?
<--- Score

2. How do you think the partners involved in Microsoft SharePoint Server would have defined success?
<--- Score

3. What is in scope?
<--- Score

4. Are required metrics defined, what are they?
<--- Score

5. Is the Microsoft SharePoint Server scope complete and appropriately sized?
<--- Score

6. Is the improvement team aware of the different versions of a process: what they think it is vs. what it actually is vs. what it should be vs. what it could be?
<--- Score

7. What is out-of-scope initially?
<--- Score

8. How does the Microsoft SharePoint Server manager ensure against scope creep?
<--- Score

9. What defines best in class?
<--- Score

10. Is Microsoft SharePoint Server required?
<--- Score

11. Has a high-level 'as is' process map been completed, verified and validated?
<--- Score

12. Are roles and responsibilities formally defined?
<--- Score

13. Is the team adequately staffed with the desired cross-functionality? If not, what additional resources are available to the team?
<--- Score

14. Are team charters developed?
<--- Score

15. What key business process output measure(s) does Microsoft SharePoint Server leverage and how?
<--- Score

16. What is the scope of Microsoft SharePoint Server?
<--- Score

17. What are the rough order estimates on cost savings/opportunities that Microsoft SharePoint Server brings?
<--- Score

18. How was the 'as is' process map developed, reviewed, verified and validated?
<--- Score

19. Is data collected and displayed to better understand customer(s) critical needs and requirements.
<--- Score

20. Who are the Microsoft SharePoint Server improvement team members, including Management Leads and Coaches?
<--- Score

21. How will the Microsoft SharePoint Server team and the organization measure complete success of

Microsoft SharePoint Server?
<--- Score

22. What is out of scope?
<--- Score

23. How can the value of Microsoft SharePoint Server be defined?
<--- Score

24. Is full participation by members in regularly held team meetings guaranteed?
<--- Score

25. How is the team tracking and documenting its work?
<--- Score

26. What are the record-keeping requirements of Microsoft SharePoint Server activities?
<--- Score

27. Are different versions of process maps needed to account for the different types of inputs?
<--- Score

28. What baselines are required to be defined and managed?
<--- Score

29. What are the compelling business reasons for embarking on Microsoft SharePoint Server?
<--- Score

30. Are improvement team members fully trained on Microsoft SharePoint Server?

<--- Score

31. What are the dynamics of the communication plan?
<--- Score

32. Is there a critical path to deliver Microsoft SharePoint Server results?
<--- Score

33. Are customer(s) identified and segmented according to their different needs and requirements?
<--- Score

34. Are there different segments of customers?
<--- Score

35. Is Microsoft SharePoint Server currently on schedule according to the plan?
<--- Score

36. Has a project plan, Gantt chart, or similar been developed/completed?
<--- Score

37. What critical content must be communicated – who, what, when, where, and how?
<--- Score

38. How and when will the baselines be defined?
<--- Score

39. What is the scope?
<--- Score

40. Will team members perform Microsoft SharePoint

Server work when assigned and in a timely fashion?
<--- Score

41. What constraints exist that might impact the team?
<--- Score

42. How often are the team meetings?
<--- Score

43. Do the problem and goal statements meet the SMART criteria (specific, measurable, attainable, relevant, and time-bound)?
<--- Score

44. Is a fully trained team formed, supported, and committed to work on the Microsoft SharePoint Server improvements?
<--- Score

45. What is the definition of success?
<--- Score

46. Have all of the relationships been defined properly?
<--- Score

47. Are audit criteria, scope, frequency and methods defined?
<--- Score

48. How do you hand over Microsoft SharePoint Server context?
<--- Score

49. When is the estimated completion date?

<--- Score

50. What scope to assess?
<--- Score

51. Is this a valid record, created by an authorized person, and required for saving?
<--- Score

52. Is there a completed, verified, and validated high-level 'as is' (not 'should be' or 'could be') business process map?
<--- Score

53. In what way can you redefine the criteria of choice clients have in your category in your favor?
<--- Score

54. Have all basic functions of Microsoft SharePoint Server been defined?
<--- Score

55. Why are you doing Microsoft SharePoint Server and what is the scope?
<--- Score

56. How did the Microsoft SharePoint Server manager receive input to the development of a Microsoft SharePoint Server improvement plan and the estimated completion dates/times of each activity?
<--- Score

57. What is the scope of the Microsoft SharePoint Server effort?
<--- Score

58. Who defines (or who defined) the rules and roles?
<--- Score

59. What system do you use for gathering Microsoft SharePoint Server information?
<--- Score

60. What are your office suite format requirements?
<--- Score

61. What Microsoft SharePoint Server requirements should be gathered?
<--- Score

62. Are customers identified and high impact areas defined?
<--- Score

63. Are accountability and ownership for Microsoft SharePoint Server clearly defined?
<--- Score

64. How do you manage scope?
<--- Score

65. What customer feedback methods were used to solicit their input?
<--- Score

66. Has/have the customer(s) been identified?
<--- Score

67. When was the Microsoft SharePoint Server start date?
<--- Score

68. Who is gathering Microsoft SharePoint Server information?
<--- Score

69. What is in the scope and what is not in scope?
<--- Score

70. Are task requirements clearly defined?
<--- Score

71. Is it clearly defined in and to your organization what you do?
<--- Score

72. What happens if Microsoft SharePoint Server's scope changes?
<--- Score

73. Has the Microsoft SharePoint Server work been fairly and/or equitably divided and delegated among team members who are qualified and capable to perform the work? Has everyone contributed?
<--- Score

74. What specifically is the problem? Where does it occur? When does it occur? What is its extent?
<--- Score

75. Is the team equipped with available and reliable resources?
<--- Score

76. Has everyone on the team, including the team leaders, been properly trained?
<--- Score

77. Is there a Microsoft SharePoint Server management charter, including business case, problem and goal statements, scope, milestones, roles and responsibilities, communication plan?
<--- Score

78. Is the current 'as is' process being followed? If not, what are the discrepancies?
<--- Score

79. Does the scope remain the same?
<--- Score

80. Is scope creep really all bad news?
<--- Score

81. Is the team formed and are team leaders (Coaches and Management Leads) assigned?
<--- Score

82. Will team members regularly document their Microsoft SharePoint Server work?
<--- Score

83. Is the Microsoft SharePoint Server scope manageable?
<--- Score

84. What was the context?
<--- Score

85. Are resources adequate for the scope?
<--- Score

86. Have specific policy objectives been defined?

<--- Score

87. What sources do you use to gather information for a Microsoft SharePoint Server study?
<--- Score

88. Has the improvement team collected the 'voice of the customer' (obtained feedback – qualitative and quantitative)?
<--- Score

89. Has a team charter been developed and communicated?
<--- Score

90. Is Microsoft SharePoint Server linked to key business goals and objectives?
<--- Score

91. Do you all define Microsoft SharePoint Server in the same way?
<--- Score

92. When are meeting minutes sent out? Who is on the distribution list?
<--- Score

93. Has the direction changed at all during the course of Microsoft SharePoint Server? If so, when did it change and why?
<--- Score

94. Are approval levels defined for contracts and supplements to contracts?
<--- Score

95. How do you gather Microsoft SharePoint Server requirements?
<--- Score

96. How do you keep key subject matter experts in the loop?
<--- Score

97. Scope of sensitive information?
<--- Score

98. What would be the goal or target for a Microsoft SharePoint Server's improvement team?
<--- Score

99. If substitutes have been appointed, have they been briefed on the Microsoft SharePoint Server goals and received regular communications as to the progress to date?
<--- Score

100. How will variation in the actual durations of each activity be dealt with to ensure that the expected Microsoft SharePoint Server results are met?
<--- Score

101. Has your scope been defined?
<--- Score

102. Has anyone else (internal or external to the organization) attempted to solve this problem or a similar one before? If so, what knowledge can be leveraged from these previous efforts?
<--- Score

103. How would you define the culture at your

organization, how susceptible is it to Microsoft SharePoint Server changes?
<--- Score

104. Are there any constraints known that bear on the ability to perform Microsoft SharePoint Server work? How is the team addressing them?
<--- Score

105. What are the Roles and Responsibilities for each team member and its leadership? Where is this documented?
<--- Score

106. Is the scope of Microsoft SharePoint Server defined?
<--- Score

107. Is there a completed SIPOC representation, describing the Suppliers, Inputs, Process, Outputs, and Customers?
<--- Score

108. Is there regularly 100% attendance at the team meetings? If not, have appointed substitutes attended to preserve cross-functionality and full representation?
<--- Score

109. Is the team sponsored by a champion or business leader?
<--- Score

110. What level of integration is required with SharePoint?
<--- Score

111. What are the tasks and definitions?
<--- Score

112. Have the customer needs been translated into specific, measurable requirements? How?
<--- Score

113. In the case that the hardware specified is not providing the desired throughput or failover capabilities, who is responsible for providing the additional equipment?
<--- Score

114. Does the team have regular meetings?
<--- Score

115. Are business processes mapped?
<--- Score

116. Is there any requirement of inbound/ outbound fax?
<--- Score

117. What is the context?
<--- Score

Add up total points for this section:
_____ = Total points for this section

Divided by: ______ (number of statements answered) = ______ Average score for this section

Transfer your score to the Microsoft SharePoint Server Index at the beginning of the Self-Assessment.

CRITERION #3: MEASURE:

INTENT: Gather the correct data. Measure the current performance and evolution of the situation.

In my belief, the answer to this question is clearly defined:

5 Strongly Agree

4 Agree

3 Neutral

2 Disagree

1 Strongly Disagree

1. How are measurements made?
<--- Score

2. What is the right balance of time and resources between investigation, analysis, and discussion and dissemination?
<--- Score

3. What could cause you to change course?

<--- Score

4. Have all non-recommended alternatives been analyzed in sufficient detail?
<--- Score

5. Have you found any 'ground fruit' or 'low-hanging fruit' for immediate remedies to the gap in performance?
<--- Score

6. What are the costs of reform?
<--- Score

7. Do you aggressively reward and promote the people who have the biggest impact on creating excellent Microsoft SharePoint Server services/products?
<--- Score

8. Among the Microsoft SharePoint Server product and service cost to be estimated, which is considered hardest to estimate?
<--- Score

9. Is the solution cost-effective?
<--- Score

10. Does Microsoft SharePoint Server analysis isolate the fundamental causes of problems?
<--- Score

11. How do you identify and analyze stakeholders and their interests?
<--- Score

12. Is long term and short term variability accounted for?
<--- Score

13. How can you measure Microsoft SharePoint Server in a systematic way?
<--- Score

14. Can you measure the return on analysis?
<--- Score

15. Is Process Variation Displayed/Communicated?
<--- Score

16. What disadvantage does this cause for the user?
<--- Score

17. What causes innovation to fail or succeed in your organization?
<--- Score

18. How will the impact of the function be evaluated?
<--- Score

19. Is it possible to estimate the impact of unanticipated complexity such as wrong or failed assumptions, feedback, etc. on proposed reforms?
<--- Score

20. How can you measure the performance?
<--- Score

21. Are there any easy-to-implement alternatives to Microsoft SharePoint Server? Sometimes other solutions are available that do not require the cost

implications of a full-blown project?
<--- Score

22. What relevant entities could be measured?
<--- Score

23. Has the impact of cost overruns been analyzed?
<--- Score

24. Why do the measurements/indicators matter?
<--- Score

25. Why do you expend time and effort to implement measurement, for whom?
<--- Score

26. Is data collected on key measures that were identified?
<--- Score

27. How do you stay flexible and focused to recognize larger Microsoft SharePoint Server results?
<--- Score

28. How frequently do you track Microsoft SharePoint Server measures?
<--- Score

29. How will you measure your Microsoft SharePoint Server effectiveness?
<--- Score

30. What data was collected (past, present, future/ongoing)?
<--- Score

31. What methods are feasible and acceptable to estimate the impact of reforms?
<--- Score

32. How will effects be measured?
<--- Score

33. Are the units of measure consistent?
<--- Score

34. How do you focus on what is right -not who is right?
<--- Score

35. Has the impact of late delivery been analyzed?
<--- Score

36. Is there a Performance Baseline?
<--- Score

37. Have changes been properly/adequately analyzed for effect?
<--- Score

38. Does Microsoft SharePoint Server analysis show the relationships among important Microsoft SharePoint Server factors?
<--- Score

39. Have the types of risks that may impact Microsoft SharePoint Server been identified and analyzed?
<--- Score

40. Is full information and analysis of users of the service available?

<--- Score

41. Is data collection planned and executed?
<--- Score

42. What harm might be caused?
<--- Score

43. What could cause delays in the schedule?
<--- Score

44. Are missed Microsoft SharePoint Server opportunities costing your organization money?
<--- Score

45. What measurements are being captured?
<--- Score

46. Do you effectively measure and reward individual and team performance?
<--- Score

47. How is the value delivered by Microsoft SharePoint Server being measured?
<--- Score

48. How do you control the overall costs of your work processes?
<--- Score

49. What are the uncertainties surrounding estimates of impact?
<--- Score

50. How do you measure success?
<--- Score

51. Are you taking your company in the direction of better and revenue or cheaper and cost?
<--- Score

52. How do you measure efficient delivery of Microsoft SharePoint Server services?
<--- Score

53. What are your key Microsoft SharePoint Server organizational performance measures, including key short and longer-term financial measures?
<--- Score

54. Does your organization systematically track and analyze outcomes related for accountability and quality improvement?
<--- Score

55. What would be a real cause for concern?
<--- Score

56. The approach of traditional Microsoft SharePoint Server works for detail complexity but is focused on a systematic approach rather than an understanding of the nature of systems themselves, what approach will permit your organization to deal with the kind of unpredictable emergent behaviors that dynamic complexity can introduce?
<--- Score

57. Are high impact defects defined and identified in the business process?
<--- Score

58. How do you know that any Microsoft SharePoint

Server analysis is complete and comprehensive?
<--- Score

59. How is performance measured?
<--- Score

60. Are you aware of what could cause a problem?
<--- Score

61. How large is the gap between current performance and the customer-specified (goal) performance?
<--- Score

62. What has the team done to assure the stability and accuracy of the measurement process?
<--- Score

63. What measurements are possible, practicable and meaningful?
<--- Score

64. What causes mismanagement?
<--- Score

65. Was a data collection plan established?
<--- Score

66. What key measures identified indicate the performance of the business process?
<--- Score

67. Can you do Microsoft SharePoint Server without complex (expensive) analysis?
<--- Score

68. Where is it measured?
<--- Score

69. Does Microsoft SharePoint Server systematically track and analyze outcomes for accountability and quality improvement?
<--- Score

70. What charts has the team used to display the components of variation in the process?
<--- Score

71. Is a solid data collection plan established that includes measurement systems analysis?
<--- Score

72. What are your customers expectations and measures?
<--- Score

73. How do you measure variability?
<--- Score

74. What are the agreed upon definitions of the high impact areas, defect(s), unit(s), and opportunities that will figure into the process capability metrics?
<--- Score

75. Who participated in the data collection for measurements?
<--- Score

76. What do you measure and why?
<--- Score

77. Which measures and indicators matter?

<--- Score

78. Who should receive measurement reports?
<--- Score

79. How do you measure lifecycle phases?
<--- Score

80. Is key measure data collection planned and executed, process variation displayed and communicated and performance baselined?
<--- Score

81. Are process variation components displayed/ communicated using suitable charts, graphs, plots?
<--- Score

82. Are key measures identified and agreed upon?
<--- Score

83. What are the types and number of measures to use?
<--- Score

84. Which stakeholder characteristics are analyzed?
<--- Score

85. What potential environmental factors impact the Microsoft SharePoint Server effort?
<--- Score

86. What is an unallowable cost?
<--- Score

87. How will success or failure be measured?
<--- Score

88. What is measured? Why?
<--- Score

89. What are your key Microsoft SharePoint Server indicators that you will measure, analyze and track?
<--- Score

90. Are the measurements objective?
<--- Score

91. Have you made assumptions about the shape of the future, particularly its impact on your customers and competitors?
<--- Score

92. Did you tackle the cause or the symptom?
<--- Score

93. What particular quality tools did the team find helpful in establishing measurements?
<--- Score

94. How is progress measured?
<--- Score

95. How to cause the change?
<--- Score

96. What are the key input variables? What are the key process variables? What are the key output variables?
<--- Score

97. Does the Microsoft SharePoint Server task fit the client's priorities?
<--- Score

98. What causes investor action?
<--- Score

99. How will measures be used to manage and adapt?
<--- Score

100. How do you do risk analysis of rare, cascading, catastrophic events?
<--- Score

101. Are there measurements based on task performance?
<--- Score

102. Are losses documented, analyzed, and remedial processes developed to prevent future losses?
<--- Score

103. How do you aggregate measures across priorities?
<--- Score

104. How do your measurements capture actionable Microsoft SharePoint Server information for use in exceeding your customers expectations and securing your customers engagement?
<--- Score

105. How will you measure success?
<--- Score

106. What causes extra work or rework?
<--- Score

107. How will your organization measure success?

<--- Score

108. What evidence is there and what is measured?
<--- Score

109. Have the concerns of stakeholders to help identify and define potential barriers been obtained and analyzed?
<--- Score

110. Do staff have the necessary skills to collect, analyze, and report data?
<--- Score

Add up total points for this section:
_____ = Total points for this section

Divided by: ______ (number of statements answered) = ______ Average score for this section

Transfer your score to the Microsoft SharePoint Server Index at the beginning of the Self-Assessment.

CRITERION #4: ANALYZE:

INTENT: Analyze causes, assumptions and hypotheses.

In my belief, the answer to this question is clearly defined:

5 Strongly Agree

4 Agree

3 Neutral

2 Disagree

1 Strongly Disagree

1. What Microsoft SharePoint Server data do you gather or use now?
<--- Score

2. Do your leaders quickly bounce back from setbacks?
<--- Score

3. What data is gathered?
<--- Score

4. Do your employees have the opportunity to do what they do best everyday?
<--- Score

5. How do you implement and manage your work processes to ensure that they meet design requirements?
<--- Score

6. What are your current levels and trends in key measures or indicators of Microsoft SharePoint Server product and process performance that are important to and directly serve your customers? How do these results compare with the performance of your competitors and other organizations with similar offerings?
<--- Score

7. What did the team gain from developing a sub-process map?
<--- Score

8. Simply delivering process information to the right users is not enough: how can you ensure that the process information is meaningful, accurate and up-to-date?
<--- Score

9. Do you, as a leader, bounce back quickly from setbacks?
<--- Score

10. Can you add value to the current Microsoft SharePoint Server decision-making process (largely qualitative) by incorporating uncertainty modeling

(more quantitative)?
<--- Score

11. Where is the data coming from to measure compliance?
<--- Score

12. Did any value-added analysis or 'lean thinking' take place to identify some of the gaps shown on the 'as is' process map?
<--- Score

13. What are the revised rough estimates of the financial savings/opportunity for Microsoft SharePoint Server improvements?
<--- Score

14. What other organizational variables, such as reward systems or communication systems, affect the performance of this Microsoft SharePoint Server process?
<--- Score

15. What tools were used to generate the list of possible causes?
<--- Score

16. Have any additional benefits been identified that will result from closing all or most of the gaps?
<--- Score

17. What controls do you have in place to protect data?
<--- Score

18. Are Microsoft SharePoint Server changes

recognized early enough to be approved through the regular process?
<--- Score

19. What were the crucial 'moments of truth' on the process map?
<--- Score

20. How do you identify specific Microsoft SharePoint Server investment opportunities and emerging trends?
<--- Score

21. What are your best practices for minimizing Microsoft SharePoint Server project risk, while demonstrating incremental value and quick wins throughout the Microsoft SharePoint Server project lifecycle?
<--- Score

22. Think about some of the processes you undertake within your organization, which do you own?
<--- Score

23. Does your application show data business owners?
<--- Score

24. What is your organizations process which leads to recognition of value generation?
<--- Score

25. What are the target business processes your organization would like to improve with this initial project?
<--- Score

26. What process should you select for improvement?
<--- Score

27. Record-keeping requirements flow from the records needed as inputs, outputs, controls and for transformation of a Microsoft SharePoint Server process. Are the records needed as inputs to the Microsoft SharePoint Server process available?
<--- Score

28. How do you use Microsoft SharePoint Server data and information to support organizational decision making and innovation?
<--- Score

29. Have the problem and goal statements been updated to reflect the additional knowledge gained from the analyze phase?
<--- Score

30. What other jobs or tasks affect the performance of the steps in the Microsoft SharePoint Server process?
<--- Score

31. Identify an operational issue in your organization. for example, could a particular task be done more quickly or more efficiently by Microsoft SharePoint Server?
<--- Score

32. Are gaps between current performance and the goal performance identified?
<--- Score

33. What is the cost of poor quality as supported by

the team's analysis?
<--- Score

34. Whats the process to create a site?
<--- Score

35. What methods do you use to gather Microsoft SharePoint Server data?
<--- Score

36. Were Pareto charts (or similar) used to portray the 'heavy hitters' (or key sources of variation)?
<--- Score

37. What are your current levels and trends in key Microsoft SharePoint Server measures or indicators of product and process performance that are important to and directly serve your customers?
<--- Score

38. How do you measure the operational performance of your key work systems and processes, including productivity, cycle time, and other appropriate measures of process effectiveness, efficiency, and innovation?
<--- Score

39. What are your Microsoft SharePoint Server processes?
<--- Score

40. Is the contractor responsible for implementing a backup strategy to minimize loss of data?
<--- Score

41. Did any additional data need to be collected?

<--- Score

42. How do mission and objectives affect the Microsoft SharePoint Server processes of your organization?
<--- Score

43. Do several people in different organizational units assist with the Microsoft SharePoint Server process?
<--- Score

44. Does your application show user permissions for files in Microsoft OneDrive?
<--- Score

45. Were any designed experiments used to generate additional insight into the data analysis?
<--- Score

46. An organizationally feasible system request is one that considers the mission, goals and objectives of the organization. Key questions are: is the Microsoft SharePoint Server solution request practical and will it solve a problem or take advantage of an opportunity to achieve company goals?
<--- Score

47. Do your applications include DLP (Data Loss Protection) capabilities?
<--- Score

48. Is the suppliers process defined and controlled?
<--- Score

49. What does the data say about the performance of the business process?

<--- Score

50. Was a detailed process map created to amplify critical steps of the 'as is' business process?
<--- Score

51. Is the Microsoft SharePoint Server process severely broken such that a re-design is necessary?
<--- Score

52. How does the organization define, manage, and improve its Microsoft SharePoint Server processes?
<--- Score

53. How was the detailed process map generated, verified, and validated?
<--- Score

54. Is there a file size limit for searching data?
<--- Score

55. What successful thing are you doing today that may be blinding you to new growth opportunities?
<--- Score

56. Does your application search files in cloud storage Microsoft OneDrive?
<--- Score

57. Is the performance gap determined?
<--- Score

58. Is Data and process analysis, root cause analysis and quantifying the gap/opportunity in place?
<--- Score

59. What were the financial benefits resulting from any 'ground fruit or low-hanging fruit' (quick fixes)?
<--- Score

60. How often will data be collected for measures?
<--- Score

61. What quality tools were used to get through the analyze phase?
<--- Score

62. Word processing applications: one or several?
<--- Score

63. Do the Shared Drives you work with follow a common Directory naming structure?
<--- Score

64. How do your work systems and key work processes relate to and capitalize on your core competencies?
<--- Score

65. Is the gap/opportunity displayed and communicated in financial terms?
<--- Score

66. Do your contracts/agreements contain data security obligations?
<--- Score

67. What will drive Microsoft SharePoint Server change?
<--- Score

68. How is Microsoft SharePoint Server data gathered?

<--- Score

69. What information (data) does the record contain?
<--- Score

70. Is the required Microsoft SharePoint Server data gathered?
<--- Score

71. Was a cause-and-effect diagram used to explore the different types of causes (or sources of variation)?
<--- Score

72. A compounding model resolution with available relevant data can often provide insight towards a solution methodology; which Microsoft SharePoint Server models, tools and techniques are necessary?
<--- Score

73. Where is Microsoft SharePoint Server data gathered?
<--- Score

74. How do you promote understanding that opportunity for improvement is not criticism of the status quo, or the people who created the status quo?
<--- Score

75. What are the best opportunities for value improvement?
<--- Score

76. What is the difference between Enterprise Information Management and Data Warehousing?
<--- Score

77. Think about the functions involved in your Microsoft SharePoint Server project, what processes flow from these functions?
<--- Score

78. What tools were used to narrow the list of possible causes?
<--- Score

79. Were there any improvement opportunities identified from the process analysis?
<--- Score

80. What are your key performance measures or indicators and in-process measures for the control and improvement of your Microsoft SharePoint Server processes?
<--- Score

81. What conclusions were drawn from the team's data collection and analysis? How did the team reach these conclusions?
<--- Score

82. How is the way you as the leader think and process information affecting your organizational culture?
<--- Score

Add up total points for this section:
_____ = Total points for this section

Divided by: ______ (number of statements answered) = ______ Average score for this section

Transfer your score to the Microsoft SharePoint Server Index at the beginning of the Self-Assessment.

CRITERION #5: IMPROVE:

INTENT: Develop a practical solution. Innovate, establish and test the solution and to measure the results.

In my belief, the answer to this question is clearly defined:

5 Strongly Agree

4 Agree

3 Neutral

2 Disagree

1 Strongly Disagree

1. Can you insist on obtaining electronic documents from a non-party?
<--- Score

2. What resources are required for the improvement efforts?
<--- Score

3. How does the team improve its work?

<--- Score

4. How do you improve your likelihood of success ?
<--- Score

5. What lessons, if any, from a pilot were incorporated into the design of the full-scale solution?
<--- Score

6. What were the underlying assumptions on the cost-benefit analysis?
<--- Score

7. For estimation problems, how do you develop an estimation statement?
<--- Score

8. What does the 'should be' process map/design look like?
<--- Score

9. How will you know that a change is an improvement?
<--- Score

10. How do you define the solutions' scope?
<--- Score

11. In the last year, how often were you unable to retrieve or view clients saved electronically scanned documents?
<--- Score

12. Does your organization intend to use Microsoft SharePoint web content management and publishing features outside of the EDM solution?

<--- Score

13. Is supporting Microsoft SharePoint Server documentation required?
<--- Score

14. Who is knowledgeable about how and where electronic documents are stored?
<--- Score

15. Produce all versions of documents (paper and electronic, MS Word and Word Perfect)?
<--- Score

16. Does your organization use Microsoft SharePoint Server (MOSS) for IT collaboration needs around the EDM solution?
<--- Score

17. What is the risk?
<--- Score

18. Have HSI methods been applied to development of all electronic and hard-copy documentation?
<--- Score

19. Who will be responsible for documenting the Microsoft SharePoint Server requirements in detail?
<--- Score

20. Is the optimal solution selected based on testing and analysis?
<--- Score

21. Will the parties scan paper documents,

producing them electronically?
<--- Score

22. How can you improve Microsoft SharePoint Server?
<--- Score

23. What improvements have been achieved?
<--- Score

24. Are there any requirements around storage design for your virtualized SharePoint solution?
<--- Score

25. Explorations of the frontiers of Microsoft SharePoint Server will help you build influence, improve Microsoft SharePoint Server, optimize decision making, and sustain change, what is your approach?
<--- Score

26. Who controls key decisions that will be made?
<--- Score

27. Who are the people involved in developing and implementing Microsoft SharePoint Server?
<--- Score

28. How do you measure improved Microsoft SharePoint Server service perception, and satisfaction?
<--- Score

29. What practices helps your organization to develop its capacity to recognize patterns?
<--- Score

30. What went well, what should change, what can improve?
<--- Score

31. To what extent does management recognize Microsoft SharePoint Server as a tool to increase the results?
<--- Score

32. Does the core financial system provide the capability to automatically prepare the formal allotment and suballotment documents and electronically distribute them to subordinate organizations?
<--- Score

33. Is the scope clearly documented?
<--- Score

34. How do you measure risk?
<--- Score

35. What communications are necessary to support the implementation of the solution?
<--- Score

36. What attendant changes will need to be made to ensure that the solution is successful?
<--- Score

37. In the past few months, what is the smallest change you have made that has had the biggest positive result? What was it about that small change that produced the large return?
<--- Score

38. What do you want to improve?
<--- Score

39. How much time do people of your organization spend with paper vs electronic documents?
<--- Score

40. Does the core financial system provide the capability to electronically image, index, store, and retrieve document reference material?
<--- Score

41. Do those selected for the Microsoft SharePoint Server team have a good general understanding of what Microsoft SharePoint Server is all about?
<--- Score

42. Can your system generate an electronic bill after the completion of a documented event?
<--- Score

43. Are improved process ('should be') maps modified based on pilot data and analysis?
<--- Score

44. Are possible solutions generated and tested?
<--- Score

45. Risk Identification: What are the possible risk events your organization faces in relation to Microsoft SharePoint Server?
<--- Score

46. How will you know when its improved?
<--- Score

47. Are new and improved process ('should be') maps developed?
<--- Score

48. Risk factors: what are the characteristics of Microsoft SharePoint Server that make it risky?
<--- Score

49. If you sent physical documents to someone before, can you now send them the documents via email?
<--- Score

50. What is the Microsoft SharePoint Server's sustainability risk?
<--- Score

51. What error proofing will be done to address some of the discrepancies observed in the 'as is' process?
<--- Score

52. Were any criteria developed to assist the team in testing and evaluating potential solutions?
<--- Score

53. Who controls the risk?
<--- Score

54. How do you link measurement and risk?
<--- Score

55. Are you assessing Microsoft SharePoint Server and risk?
<--- Score

56. Who will be responsible for making the decisions to include or exclude requested changes once Microsoft SharePoint Server is underway?
<--- Score

57. If you could go back in time five years, what decision would you make differently? What is your best guess as to what decision you're making today you might regret five years from now?
<--- Score

58. Is the implementation plan designed?
<--- Score

59. When are electronic documents admissible evidence in the courts of law?
<--- Score

60. Is pilot data collected and analyzed?
<--- Score

61. How will you measure the results?
<--- Score

62. With what kind of activities are electronic documents used?
<--- Score

63. Can the solution be designed and implemented within an acceptable time period?
<--- Score

64. How will the team or the process owner(s) monitor the implementation plan to see that it is working as intended?
<--- Score

65. What tools were used to evaluate the potential solutions?
<--- Score

66. What are your current levels and trends in key measures or indicators of workforce and leader development?
<--- Score

67. What is the implementation plan?
<--- Score

68. How does the solution remove the key sources of issues discovered in the analyze phase?
<--- Score

69. Is your organization looking for Microsoft SharePoint to be a read only consumption model, or a creation model for documents as well?
<--- Score

70. How did the team generate the list of possible solutions?
<--- Score

71. Who will be using the results of the measurement activities?
<--- Score

72. Can you identify any significant risks or exposures to Microsoft SharePoint Server third- parties (vendors, service providers, alliance partners etc) that concern you?
<--- Score

73. Is a solution implementation plan established, including schedule/work breakdown structure, resources, risk management plan, cost/budget, and control plan?
<--- Score

74. What actually has to improve and by how much?
<--- Score

75. Is the solution technically practical?
<--- Score

76. Is there a high likelihood that any recommendations will achieve their intended results?
<--- Score

77. How do you improve Microsoft SharePoint Server service perception, and satisfaction?
<--- Score

78. Necessary documentation identified (electronic and hard copy), locations defined & stored in correct place?
<--- Score

79. Will the controls trigger any other risks?
<--- Score

80. What to do with the results or outcomes of measurements?
<--- Score

81. How can you improve performance?
<--- Score

82. For decision problems, how do you develop a

decision statement?
<--- Score

83. What is the team's contingency plan for potential problems occurring in implementation?
<--- Score

84. Is there a small-scale pilot for proposed improvement(s)? What conclusions were drawn from the outcomes of a pilot?
<--- Score

85. How will the organization know that the solution worked?
<--- Score

86. What is Microsoft SharePoint Server's impact on utilizing the best solution(s)?
<--- Score

87. Is there a cost/benefit analysis of optimal solution(s)?
<--- Score

88. Are the best solutions selected?
<--- Score

89. Does the goal represent a desired result that can be measured?
<--- Score

90. Why improve in the first place?
<--- Score

91. How significant is the improvement in the eyes of the end user?

<--- Score

92. How do you manage and improve your Microsoft SharePoint Server work systems to deliver customer value and achieve organizational success and sustainability?
<--- Score

93. How can skill-level changes improve Microsoft SharePoint Server?
<--- Score

94. Is the measure of success for Microsoft SharePoint Server understandable to a variety of people?
<--- Score

95. Is a contingency plan established?
<--- Score

96. How do the Microsoft SharePoint Server results compare with the performance of your competitors and other organizations with similar offerings?
<--- Score

97. What is the magnitude of the improvements?
<--- Score

98. How do you go about comparing Microsoft SharePoint Server approaches/solutions?
<--- Score

99. Describe the design of the pilot and what tests were conducted, if any?
<--- Score

100. Do you currently use a scanner to save client

documents electronically?
<--- Score

101. Are there any constraints (technical, political, cultural, or otherwise) that would inhibit certain solutions?
<--- Score

102. So how should documents be distributed?
<--- Score

103. Which of the recognised risks out of all risks can be most likely transferred?
<--- Score

104. How do you improve productivity?
<--- Score

105. What tools were used to tap into the creativity and encourage 'outside the box' thinking?
<--- Score

106. How will you know that you have improved?
<--- Score

107. What tools were most useful during the improve phase?
<--- Score

108. What are the implications of the one critical Microsoft SharePoint Server decision 10 minutes, 10 months, and 10 years from now?
<--- Score

109. Risk events: what are the things that could go wrong?

<--- Score

110. What needs improvement? Why?
<--- Score

111. How do you measure progress and evaluate training effectiveness?
<--- Score

112. What can you do to improve?
<--- Score

113. How do you keep improving Microsoft SharePoint Server?
<--- Score

114. Do the document production requirements allow for documents to be produced electronically such as TIFF or Native formats (especially for large attachments)?
<--- Score

115. Was a pilot designed for the proposed solution(s)?
<--- Score

116. Are risk triggers captured?
<--- Score

Add up total points for this section:
_____ = Total points for this section

Divided by: ______ (number of statements answered) = ______
Average score for this section

Transfer your score to the Microsoft SharePoint Server Index at the beginning of the Self-Assessment.

CRITERION #6: CONTROL:

INTENT: Implement the practical solution. Maintain the performance and correct possible complications.

In my belief, the answer to this question is clearly defined:

5 Strongly Agree

4 Agree

3 Neutral

2 Disagree

1 Strongly Disagree

1. In the case of a Microsoft SharePoint Server project, the criteria for the audit derive from implementation objectives. an audit of a Microsoft SharePoint Server project involves assessing whether the recommendations outlined for implementation have been met. Can you track that any Microsoft SharePoint Server project is implemented as planned, and is it working?
<--- Score

2. How do you select, collect, align, and integrate Microsoft SharePoint Server data and information for tracking daily operations and overall organizational performance, including progress relative to strategic objectives and action plans?
<--- Score

3. Are new process steps, standards, and documentation ingrained into normal operations?
<--- Score

4. Are the planned controls in place?
<--- Score

5. Is there documentation that will support the successful operation of the improvement?
<--- Score

6. How do your controls stack up?
<--- Score

7. Are the planned controls working?
<--- Score

8. What other systems, operations, processes, and infrastructures (hiring practices, staffing, training, incentives/rewards, metrics/dashboards/scorecards, etc.) need updates, additions, changes, or deletions in order to facilitate knowledge transfer and improvements?
<--- Score

9. What is the recommended frequency of auditing?
<--- Score

10. What key inputs and outputs are being measured on an ongoing basis?
<--- Score

11. What do your reports reflect?
<--- Score

12. Does a troubleshooting guide exist or is it needed?
<--- Score

13. Are suggested corrective/restorative actions indicated on the response plan for known causes to problems that might surface?
<--- Score

14. Where: Location and Control?
<--- Score

15. What are the key elements of your Microsoft SharePoint Server performance improvement system, including your evaluation, organizational learning, and innovation processes?
<--- Score

16. How will the day-to-day responsibilities for monitoring and continual improvement be transferred from the improvement team to the process owner?
<--- Score

17. How do you encourage people to take control and responsibility?
<--- Score

18. Who controls critical resources?
<--- Score

19. What can you control?
<--- Score

20. Is a response plan in place for when the input, process, or output measures indicate an 'out-of-control' condition?
<--- Score

21. Is reporting being used or needed?
<--- Score

22. Implementation Planning: is a pilot needed to test the changes before a full roll out occurs?
<--- Score

23. Are documented procedures clear and easy to follow for the operators?
<--- Score

24. What are you attempting to measure/monitor?
<--- Score

25. Does the Microsoft SharePoint Server performance meet the customer's requirements?
<--- Score

26. Are operating procedures consistent?
<--- Score

27. Will your goals reflect your program budget?
<--- Score

28. How will the process owner and team be able to hold the gains?
<--- Score

29. What is the best design framework for Microsoft SharePoint Server organization now that, in a post industrial-age if the top-down, command and control model is no longer relevant?
<--- Score

30. What do you measure to verify effectiveness gains?
<--- Score

31. Has the improved process and its steps been standardized?
<--- Score

32. How do controls support value?
<--- Score

33. Are pertinent alerts monitored, analyzed and distributed to appropriate personnel?
<--- Score

34. Who sets the Microsoft SharePoint Server standards?
<--- Score

35. How is change control managed?
<--- Score

36. How will input, process, and output variables be checked to detect for sub-optimal conditions?
<--- Score

37. Is there a control plan in place for sustaining improvements (short and long-term)?
<--- Score

38. What adjustments to the strategies are needed?
<--- Score

39. Does job training on the documented procedures need to be part of the process team's education and training?
<--- Score

40. What are the Standards for Creating and Managing Electronic Records?
<--- Score

41. What is the control/monitoring plan?
<--- Score

42. How do you establish and deploy modified action plans if circumstances require a shift in plans and rapid execution of new plans?
<--- Score

43. How will the process owner verify improvement in present and future sigma levels, process capabilities?
<--- Score

44. Have new or revised work instructions resulted?
<--- Score

45. What are the critical parameters to watch?
<--- Score

46. Is there a Microsoft SharePoint Server Communication plan covering who needs to get what information when?
<--- Score

47. How can you best use all of your knowledge repositories to enhance learning and sharing?
<--- Score

48. Who will be in control?
<--- Score

49. Will any special training be provided for results interpretation?
<--- Score

50. How do you ensure interoperability among electronic business document standards?
<--- Score

51. How do senior leaders actions reflect a commitment to the organizations Microsoft SharePoint Server values?
<--- Score

52. What quality tools were useful in the control phase?
<--- Score

53. How will new or emerging customer needs/ requirements be checked/communicated to orient the process toward meeting the new specifications and continually reducing variation?
<--- Score

54. How will the function be monitored?
<--- Score

55. The effect of organizational factors on the effectiveness of EMR system implementation--what have you learned?

<--- Score

56. Against what alternative is success being measured?
<--- Score

57. What do you stand for--and what are you against?
<--- Score

58. Are you measuring, monitoring and predicting Microsoft SharePoint Server activities to optimize operations and profitability, and enhancing outcomes?
<--- Score

59. Is knowledge gained on process shared and institutionalized?
<--- Score

60. How likely is the current Microsoft SharePoint Server plan to come in on schedule or on budget?
<--- Score

61. Where do ideas that reach policy makers and planners as proposals for Microsoft SharePoint Server strengthening and reform actually originate?
<--- Score

62. What is your theory of human motivation, and how does your compensation plan fit with that view?
<--- Score

63. What should you measure to verify efficiency gains?
<--- Score

64. Is new knowledge gained imbedded in the response plan?
<--- Score

65. What are the known security controls?
<--- Score

66. Is there a documented and implemented monitoring plan?
<--- Score

67. Act/Adjust: What Do you Need to Do Differently?
<--- Score

68. Do you monitor the Microsoft SharePoint Server decisions made and fine tune them as they evolve?
<--- Score

69. Do you monitor the effectiveness of your Microsoft SharePoint Server activities?
<--- Score

70. How will you measure your QA plan's effectiveness?
<--- Score

71. Who is the Microsoft SharePoint Server process owner?
<--- Score

72. Will the team be available to assist members in planning investigations?
<--- Score

73. Do the Microsoft SharePoint Server decisions you make today help people and the planet tomorrow?

<--- Score

74. Is the document/deliverable developed per the appropriate or required standards (for example, Institute of Electrical and Electronics Engineers standards)?
<--- Score

75. Can support from partners be adjusted?
<--- Score

76. Are controls in place and consistently applied?
<--- Score

77. Is there a transfer of ownership and knowledge to process owner and process team tasked with the responsibilities.
<--- Score

78. What other areas of the organization might benefit from the Microsoft SharePoint Server team's improvements, knowledge, and learning?
<--- Score

79. Is there a recommended audit plan for routine surveillance inspections of Microsoft SharePoint Server's gains?
<--- Score

80. Does Microsoft SharePoint Server appropriately measure and monitor risk?
<--- Score

81. You may have created your quality measures at a time when you lacked resources, technology wasn't up to the required standard, or low service levels

were the industry norm. Have those circumstances changed?
<--- Score

82. Is there a standardized process?
<--- Score

83. How do you plan on providing proper recognition and disclosure of supporting companies?
<--- Score

84. Is a response plan established and deployed?
<--- Score

85. How might the organization capture best practices and lessons learned so as to leverage improvements across the business?
<--- Score

86. As part of a governance plan, did you determine who does what? For example, who creates sites, who controls keywords in Search, or who manages the metadata and ensures that the metadata is applied correctly?
<--- Score

87. Can you adapt and adjust to changing Microsoft SharePoint Server situations?
<--- Score

88. Who has control over resources?
<--- Score

89. Does the response plan contain a definite closed loop continual improvement scheme (e.g., plan-do-check-act)?

<--- Score

90. Does the folder structure used to store electronic documents meet the organizations standards?
<--- Score

91. What should the next improvement project be that is related to Microsoft SharePoint Server?
<--- Score

92. How will report readings be checked to effectively monitor performance?
<--- Score

93. Are there documented procedures?
<--- Score

Add up total points for this section:
_____ = Total points for this section

Divided by: ______ (number of statements answered) = ______ Average score for this section

Transfer your score to the Microsoft SharePoint Server Index at the beginning of the Self-Assessment.

CRITERION #7: SUSTAIN:

INTENT: Retain the benefits.

In my belief, the answer to this question is clearly defined:

5 Strongly Agree

4 Agree

3 Neutral

2 Disagree

1 Strongly Disagree

1. If there were zero limitations, what would you do differently?
<--- Score

2. How do you determine the key elements that affect Microsoft SharePoint Server workforce satisfaction, how are these elements determined for different workforce groups and segments?
<--- Score

3. Is there a work around that you can use?

<--- Score

4. Are assumptions made in Microsoft SharePoint Server stated explicitly?
<--- Score

5. Who will provide the final approval of Microsoft SharePoint Server deliverables?
<--- Score

6. What happens at your organization when people fail?
<--- Score

7. How do you lead with Microsoft SharePoint Server in mind?
<--- Score

8. Are there bandwidth considerations for large enterprises (60,000+ users) moving entirely to the full O365 cloud service?
<--- Score

9. Are you maintaining a past–present–future perspective throughout the Microsoft SharePoint Server discussion?
<--- Score

10. Are there records on the records retention schedule?
<--- Score

11. Will it be accepted by users?
<--- Score

12. How can you become more high-tech but still be

high touch?
<--- Score

13. Where can you break convention?
<--- Score

14. What is your formula for success in Microsoft SharePoint Server ?
<--- Score

15. Does the project support your core businesses?
<--- Score

16. Political -is anyone trying to undermine this project?
<--- Score

17. What are the infrastructure constraints?
<--- Score

18. Have new benefits been realized?
<--- Score

19. Who created the record, when, why and for what purpose?
<--- Score

20. How important is Microsoft SharePoint Server to the user organizations mission?
<--- Score

21. Who have you, as a company, historically been when you've been at your best?
<--- Score

22. How Long Must Electronic Records Be Kept?

<--- Score

23. Is the impact that Microsoft SharePoint Server has shown?
<--- Score

24. If no one would ever find out about your accomplishments, how would you lead differently?
<--- Score

25. Is it economical; do you have the time and money?
<--- Score

26. How can you incorporate support to ensure safe and effective use of Microsoft SharePoint Server into the services that you provide?
<--- Score

27. Why is it important to have senior management support for a Microsoft SharePoint Server project?
<--- Score

28. What is effective Microsoft SharePoint Server?
<--- Score

29. What may be the consequences for the performance of an organization if all stakeholders are not consulted regarding Microsoft SharePoint Server?
<--- Score

30. How do you cross-sell and up-sell your Microsoft SharePoint Server success?
<--- Score

31. Is Microsoft SharePoint Server dependent on the successful delivery of a current project?

<--- Score

32. How many MOSS front ends does the organization currently have?
<--- Score

33. What are the business goals Microsoft SharePoint Server is aiming to achieve?
<--- Score

34. Are there any activities that you can take off your to do list?
<--- Score

35. What is the kind of project structure that would be appropriate for your Microsoft SharePoint Server project, should it be formal and complex, or can it be less formal and relatively simple?
<--- Score

36. To whom do you add value?
<--- Score

37. How much does Microsoft SharePoint Server help?
<--- Score

38. Who are the key stakeholders?
<--- Score

39. What is your Electronic Records Retention?
<--- Score

40. Will there be any necessary staff changes (redundancies or new hires)?
<--- Score

41. How many client access licenses (CALs) does the organization own for MOSS Enterprise?
<--- Score

42. Does upper management support the project effort?
<--- Score

43. How are you doing compared to your industry?
<--- Score

44. How can or do licenses/subscriptions transfer?
<--- Score

45. How do you foster innovation?
<--- Score

46. How do you target content to specific audiences?
<--- Score

47. How will you insure seamless interoperability of Microsoft SharePoint Server moving forward?
<--- Score

48. Who else should you help?
<--- Score

49. Who do you think the world wants your organization to be?
<--- Score

50. Is it the complete (correct, current) version?
<--- Score

51. Have benefits been optimized with all key

stakeholders?
<--- Score

52. Who do we want your customers to become?
<--- Score

53. Do you say no to customers for no reason?
<--- Score

54. How do you deal with Microsoft SharePoint Server changes?
<--- Score

55. What is the craziest thing you can do?
<--- Score

56. How can you negotiate Microsoft SharePoint Server successfully with a stubborn boss, an irate client, or a deceitful coworker?
<--- Score

57. Is your basic point _____ or _____?
<--- Score

58. What are the long-term Microsoft SharePoint Server goals?
<--- Score

59. Are all key stakeholders present at all Structured Walkthroughs?
<--- Score

60. Who do you want your customers to become?
<--- Score

61. How will you motivate the stakeholders with the

least vested interest?
<--- Score

62. What does your signature ensure?
<--- Score

63. Who are your customers?
<--- Score

64. What should you stop doing?
<--- Score

65. Were lessons learned captured and communicated?
<--- Score

66. What are specific Microsoft SharePoint Server rules to follow?
<--- Score

67. How do you stay inspired?
<--- Score

68. Do you have past Microsoft SharePoint Server successes?
<--- Score

69. If you had to leave your organization for a year and the only communication you could have with employees/colleagues was a single paragraph, what would you write?
<--- Score

70. What would you recommend your friend do if he/she were facing this dilemma?
<--- Score

71. Are the criteria for selecting recommendations stated?
<--- Score

72. How do you maintain Microsoft SharePoint Server's Integrity?
<--- Score

73. How much information?
<--- Score

74. Why not do Microsoft SharePoint Server?
<--- Score

75. Do you think you know, or do you know you know ?
<--- Score

76. How do you foster the skills, knowledge, talents, attributes, and characteristics you want to have?
<--- Score

77. Do you see more potential in people than they do in themselves?
<--- Score

78. What is the range of capabilities?
<--- Score

79. Whose voice (department, ethnic group, women, older workers, etc) might you have missed hearing from in your company, and how might you amplify this voice to create positive momentum for your business?
<--- Score

80. Is this the right tool?
<--- Score

81. Ask yourself: how would you do this work if you only had one staff member to do it?
<--- Score

82. Does your application show user permissions for files in SharePoint Online?
<--- Score

83. Are there any disadvantages to implementing Microsoft SharePoint Server? There might be some that are less obvious?
<--- Score

84. How do you transition from the baseline to the target?
<--- Score

85. Do you have the resources?
<--- Score

86. What current systems have to be understood and/or changed?
<--- Score

87. What is an Electronic Record?
<--- Score

88. Do you have enough freaky customers in your portfolio pushing you to the limit day in and day out?
<--- Score

89. Does any application have any insider threat

detection and response capability?
<--- Score

90. What is the recommended frequency of auditing?
<--- Score

91. What are you trying to prove to yourself, and how might it be hijacking your life and business success?
<--- Score

92. Did your employees make progress today?
<--- Score

93. If your company went out of business tomorrow, would anyone who doesn't get a paycheck here care?
<--- Score

94. How do you proactively clarify deliverables and Microsoft SharePoint Server quality expectations?
<--- Score

95. What are internal and external Microsoft SharePoint Server relations?
<--- Score

96. What are your most important goals for the strategic Microsoft SharePoint Server objectives?
<--- Score

97. How do you decide how much to remunerate an employee?
<--- Score

98. What is the purpose of Microsoft SharePoint Server in relation to the mission?
<--- Score

99. What information is critical to your organization that your executives are ignoring?
<--- Score

100. Are you using Microsoft SharePoint as an interface for Enterprise Applications?
<--- Score

101. How do you make it meaningful in connecting Microsoft SharePoint Server with what users do day-to-day?
<--- Score

102. What are the key enablers to make this Microsoft SharePoint Server move?
<--- Score

103. What is an unauthorized commitment?
<--- Score

104. Who is the main stakeholder, with ultimate responsibility for driving Microsoft SharePoint Server forward?
<--- Score

105. What did you miss in the interview for the worst hire you ever made?
<--- Score

106. Do you have the right capabilities and capacities?
<--- Score

107. Are you / should you be revolutionary or evolutionary?
<--- Score

108. What is the funding source for this project?
<--- Score

109. What are the challenges?
<--- Score

110. Is the Microsoft SharePoint Server organization completing tasks effectively and efficiently?
<--- Score

111. How will you know that the Microsoft SharePoint Server project has been successful?
<--- Score

112. Why will customers want to buy your organizations products/services?
<--- Score

113. What are the Rules Governing Your Organizations Creation and Management of Electronic Records?
<--- Score

114. What are the potential basics of Microsoft SharePoint Server fraud?
<--- Score

115. Which functions and people interact with the supplier and or customer?
<--- Score

116. What is an Electronic Notary Seal?
<--- Score

117. How do you go about completing an

upgrade?
<--- Score

118. Is a Microsoft SharePoint Server team work effort in place?
<--- Score

119. What are the gaps in your knowledge and experience?
<--- Score

120. What management system can you use to leverage the Microsoft SharePoint Server experience, ideas, and concerns of the people closest to the work to be done?
<--- Score

121. Can you maintain your growth without detracting from the factors that have contributed to your success?
<--- Score

122. Do Microsoft SharePoint Server rules make a reasonable demand on a users capabilities?
<--- Score

123. Why Destroy Records?
<--- Score

124. How do you structure permissions in a site?
<--- Score

125. How do you go about securing Microsoft SharePoint Server?
<--- Score

126. What is it like to work for you?
<--- Score

127. When information truly is ubiquitous, when reach and connectivity are completely global, when computing resources are infinite, and when a whole new set of impossibilities are not only possible, but happening, what will that do to your business?
<--- Score

128. What is the source of the strategies for Microsoft SharePoint Server strengthening and reform?
<--- Score

129. What is Information?
<--- Score

130. What will be the consequences to the stakeholder (financial, reputation etc) if Microsoft SharePoint Server does not go ahead or fails to deliver the objectives?
<--- Score

131. How is implementation research currently incorporated into each of your goals?
<--- Score

132. What must you excel at?
<--- Score

133. In the past year, what have you done (or could you have done) to increase the accurate perception of your company/brand as ethical and honest?
<--- Score

134. How will you ensure you get what you expected?

<--- Score

135. What is your BATNA (best alternative to a negotiated agreement)?
<--- Score

136. Can two internal approvals be reduced to one?
<--- Score

137. Do you think Microsoft SharePoint Server accomplishes the goals you expect it to accomplish?
<--- Score

138. Is this a vital record?
<--- Score

139. What Microsoft SharePoint Server modifications can you make work for you?
<--- Score

140. What Microsoft SharePoint Server skills are most important?
<--- Score

141. What are the success criteria that will indicate that Microsoft SharePoint Server objectives have been met and the benefits delivered?
<--- Score

142. Has implementation been effective in reaching specified objectives so far?
<--- Score

143. Why should you adopt a Microsoft SharePoint Server framework?

<--- Score

144. What is the exit strategy to leave O365?
<--- Score

145. What was the last experiment you ran?
<--- Score

146. How do you engage the workforce, in addition to satisfying them?
<--- Score

147. What role does communication play in the success or failure of a Microsoft SharePoint Server project?
<--- Score

148. Do you know what you are doing? And who do you call if you don't?
<--- Score

149. How do you dispose of electronic records?
<--- Score

150. What are current Microsoft SharePoint Server paradigms?
<--- Score

151. How do you govern and fulfill your societal responsibilities?
<--- Score

152. Is Microsoft SharePoint Server realistic, or are you setting yourself up for failure?
<--- Score

153. How do you assess the Microsoft SharePoint Server pitfalls that are inherent in implementing it?
<--- Score

154. What happens when a new employee joins the organization?
<--- Score

155. What do we do when new problems arise?
<--- Score

156. Implementing EDRM: has it provided the benefits expected?
<--- Score

157. When you map the key players in your own work and the types/domains of relationships with them, which relationships do you find easy and which challenging, and why?
<--- Score

158. What goals did you miss?
<--- Score

159. How much contingency will be available in the budget?
<--- Score

160. In a project to restructure Microsoft SharePoint Server outcomes, which stakeholders would you involve?
<--- Score

161. How likely is it that a customer would recommend your company to a friend or colleague?
<--- Score

162. If your customer were your grandmother, would you tell her to buy what you're selling?
<--- Score

163. What trouble can you get into?
<--- Score

164. Who are four people whose careers you have enhanced?
<--- Score

165. If you weren't already in this business, would you enter it today? And if not, what are you going to do about it?
<--- Score

166. Who is responsible for errors?
<--- Score

167. What happens if you do not have enough funding?
<--- Score

168. What are strategies for increasing support and reducing opposition?
<--- Score

169. How do you keep the momentum going?
<--- Score

170. This program will ensure you will design, implement, upgrade or manage your DMS/EDMS/TDMS systems?
<--- Score

171. How do you provide a safe environment -physically and emotionally?
<--- Score

172. What consultation has taken place?
<--- Score

173. Think of your Microsoft SharePoint Server project, what are the main functions?
<--- Score

174. How does Microsoft SharePoint Server integrate with other business initiatives?
<--- Score

175. Whom among your colleagues do you trust, and for what?
<--- Score

176. How long will it take to change?
<--- Score

177. What counts that you are not counting?
<--- Score

178. How do you create buy-in?
<--- Score

179. If you got fired and a new hire took your place, what would she do different?
<--- Score

180. How does your organization approach the SharePoint Deployment Conundrum: On-premises, Cloud or Hybrid?
<--- Score

181. What are the rules and assumptions your industry operates under? What if the opposite were true?
<--- Score

182. What would have to be true for the option on the table to be the best possible choice?
<--- Score

183. What one word do you want to own in the minds of your customers, employees, and partners?
<--- Score

184. Are the assumptions believable and achievable?
<--- Score

185. Why compress?
<--- Score

186. Who is on the team?
<--- Score

187. What is your competitive advantage?
<--- Score

188. Original or duplicate copy?
<--- Score

189. What are the barriers to increased Microsoft SharePoint Server production?
<--- Score

190. Which authentication mechanism do you use?
<--- Score

191. Who uses your product in ways you never

expected?
<--- Score

192. Characteristics of Records?
<--- Score

193. What are the essentials of internal Microsoft SharePoint Server management?
<--- Score

194. Can you break it down?
<--- Score

195. What relationships among Microsoft SharePoint Server trends do you perceive?
<--- Score

196. Who is responsible for Microsoft SharePoint Server?
<--- Score

197. Who will be responsible for deciding whether Microsoft SharePoint Server goes ahead or not after the initial investigations?
<--- Score

198. Which individuals, teams or departments will be involved in Microsoft SharePoint Server?
<--- Score

199. What have been your experiences in defining long range Microsoft SharePoint Server goals?
<--- Score

200. Can your application create specific accounts for people with no administrative rights (external

auditors, non-IT executives, etc.), allowing them to perform audits securely and autonomously?
<--- Score

201. What are your personal philosophies regarding Microsoft SharePoint Server and how do they influence your work?
<--- Score

202. Are there benefits to your organization to pursue a single procurement for Microsoft licenses rather than separate purchases under separate EAs?
<--- Score

203. When a user gets stuck, who do they call?
<--- Score

204. Are there existing infrastructures that are serving as a barrier?
<--- Score

205. What information in the system is PII?
<--- Score

206. Are you paying enough attention to the partners your company depends on to succeed?
<--- Score

207. Who, on the executive team or the board, has spoken to a customer recently?
<--- Score

208. Why is Microsoft SharePoint Server important for you now?
<--- Score

209. Why do and why don't your customers like your organization?
<--- Score

210. What threat is Microsoft SharePoint Server addressing?
<--- Score

211. Who performs the service?
<--- Score

212. Is there any reason to believe the opposite of my current belief?
<--- Score

213. How do you manage Microsoft SharePoint Server Knowledge Management (KM)?
<--- Score

214. What stupid rule would you most like to kill?
<--- Score

215. What outcomes are wanted from this function?
<--- Score

216. What knowledge, skills and characteristics mark a good Microsoft SharePoint Server project manager?
<--- Score

217. Are you changing as fast as the world around you?
<--- Score

218. What are the top 3 things at the forefront of your

Microsoft SharePoint Server agendas for the next 3 years?
<--- Score

219. Are new benefits received and understood?
<--- Score

220. What projects are going on in the organization today, and what resources are those projects using from the resource pools?
<--- Score

221. What is something you believe that nearly no one agrees with you on?
<--- Score

222. Are you relevant? Will you be relevant five years from now? Ten?
<--- Score

223. What factors/forces could contribute/detract from the outcomes?
<--- Score

224. Who is responsible for managing the organization s account?
<--- Score

225. What you are going to do to affect the numbers?
<--- Score

226. How do you listen to customers to obtain actionable information?
<--- Score

227. Do you have an implicit bias for capital

investments over people investments?
<--- Score

228. Who will determine interim and final deadlines?
<--- Score

229. How do you ensure that implementations of Microsoft SharePoint Server products are done in a way that ensures safety?
<--- Score

230. If cutbacks in existing services are necessary, which services should be eliminated first?
<--- Score

231. What is a feasible sequencing of reform initiatives over time?
<--- Score

232. Are you using a design thinking approach and integrating Innovation, Microsoft SharePoint Server Experience, and Brand Value?
<--- Score

233. How do customers see your organization?
<--- Score

234. Who is responsible for ensuring appropriate resources (time, people and money) are allocated to Microsoft SharePoint Server?
<--- Score

235. Who will manage the integration of tools?
<--- Score

236. What is the organization attempting to

communicate?
<--- Score

237. How do you minimize your use of sensitive PII?
<--- Score

238. Which Microsoft SharePoint Server goals are the most important?
<--- Score

239. Does the SharePoint portal use an existing single sign-on system like LDAP or Active Directory?
<--- Score

240. How do you accomplish your long range Microsoft SharePoint Server goals?
<--- Score

241. Would you rather sell to knowledgeable and informed customers or to uninformed customers?
<--- Score

242. Where is all this information going to be kept?
<--- Score

243. What are the Rules Governing State Agencies Creation and Management of Electronic Records?
<--- Score

244. Is maximizing Microsoft SharePoint Server protection the same as minimizing Microsoft SharePoint Server loss?
<--- Score

245. At what moment would you think; Will I get fired?
<--- Score

246. In retrospect, of the projects that you pulled the plug on, what percent do you wish had been allowed to keep going, and what percent do you wish had ended earlier?
<--- Score

247. What new services of functionality will be implemented next with Microsoft SharePoint Server ?
<--- Score

248. Are you satisfied with your current role? If not, what is missing from it?
<--- Score

249. How do you track customer value, profitability or financial return, organizational success, and sustainability?
<--- Score

250. What have you done to protect your business from competitive encroachment?
<--- Score

251. Can you do all this work?
<--- Score

252. Do you have the right people on the bus?
<--- Score

253. Operational - will it work?
<--- Score

254. Marketing budgets are tighter, consumers are

more skeptical, and social media has changed forever the way we talk about Microsoft SharePoint Server. How do you gain traction?
<--- Score

255. Are you making progress, and are you making progress as Microsoft SharePoint Server leaders?
<--- Score

256. What is your question? Why?
<--- Score

257. Can the schedule be done in the given time?
<--- Score

258. Why should people listen to you?
<--- Score

259. What are the business pain points?
<--- Score

260. How do you know if you are successful?
<--- Score

261. What are the usability implications of Microsoft SharePoint Server actions?
<--- Score

262. What are the short and long-term Microsoft SharePoint Server goals?
<--- Score

263. Do you feel that more should be done in the Microsoft SharePoint Server area?
<--- Score

264. Are your responses positive or negative?
<--- Score

265. Instead of going to current contacts for new ideas, what if you reconnected with dormant contacts--the people you used to know? If you were going reactivate a dormant tie, who would it be?
<--- Score

266. If you were responsible for initiating and implementing major changes in your organization, what steps might you take to ensure acceptance of those changes?
<--- Score

267. If you do not follow, then how to lead?
<--- Score

268. Is the user's business environment stable?
<--- Score

269. Which models, tools and techniques are necessary?
<--- Score

270. What is the estimated value of the project?
<--- Score

271. Which languages will be installed and supported?
<--- Score

272. What are you challenging?
<--- Score

273. What unique value proposition (UVP) do you

offer?
<--- Score

274. What business benefits will Microsoft SharePoint Server goals deliver if achieved?
<--- Score

275. What trophy do you want on your mantle?
<--- Score

276. Who determines governance policies?
<--- Score

277. How do you keep records, of what?
<--- Score

278. What is the current number of deployed SharePoint users across the enterprise?
<--- Score

279. What kind of crime could a potential new hire have committed that would not only not disqualify him/her from being hired by your organization, but would actually indicate that he/she might be a particularly good fit?
<--- Score

280. How do you set Microsoft SharePoint Server stretch targets and how do you get people to not only participate in setting these stretch targets but also that they strive to achieve these?
<--- Score

281. What potential megatrends could make your business model obsolete?
<--- Score

282. How can you become the company that would put you out of business?
<--- Score

Add up total points for this section:
_____ = Total points for this section

Divided by: ______ (number of statements answered) = ______ Average score for this section

Transfer your score to the Microsoft SharePoint Server Index at the beginning of the Self-Assessment.

Microsoft SharePoint Server and Managing Projects, Criteria for Project Managers:

1.0 Initiating Process Group: Microsoft SharePoint Server

1. What business situation is being addressed?

2. Based on your Microsoft SharePoint Server project communication management plan, what worked well?

3. How can you make your needs known?

4. What are the constraints?

5. What will you do to minimize the impact should a risk event occur?

6. Who does what?

7. Are identified risks being monitored properly, are new risks arising during the Microsoft SharePoint Server project or are foreseen risks occurring?

8. How will you do it?

9. Were resources available as planned?

10. What were the challenges that you encountered during the execution of a previous Microsoft SharePoint Server project that you would not want to repeat?

11. Which of six sigmas dmaic phases focuses on the measurement of internal process that affect factors that are critical to quality?

12. What is the NEXT thing to do?

13. What areas were overlooked on this Microsoft SharePoint Server project?

14. What are the inputs required to produce the deliverables?

15. How to control and approve each phase?

16. Have the stakeholders identified all individual requirements pertaining to business process?

17. Specific - is the objective clear in terms of what, how, when, and where the situation will be changed?

18. Does it make any difference if you am successful?

19. How well did you do?

20. Were sponsors and decision makers available when needed outside regularly scheduled meetings?

1.1 Project Charter: Microsoft SharePoint Server

21. Who are the stakeholders?

22. When is a charter needed?

23. When do you use a Microsoft SharePoint Server project Charter?

24. Will this replace an existing product?

25. How will you learn more about the process or system you are trying to improve?

26. Why executive support?

27. What are the deliverables?

28. Is it an improvement over existing products?

29. What are you striving to accomplish (measurable goal(s))?

30. Pop quiz – which are the same inputs as in the Microsoft SharePoint Server project charter?

31. Major high-level milestone targets: what events measure progress?

32. Microsoft SharePoint Server project background: what is the primary motivation for this Microsoft SharePoint Server project?

33. How are Microsoft SharePoint Server projects different from operations?

34. Who manages integration?

35. Microsoft SharePoint Server project deliverables: what is the Microsoft SharePoint Server project going to produce?

36. How high should you set your goals?

37. Did your Microsoft SharePoint Server project ask for this?

38. What date will the task finish?

39. Why use a Microsoft SharePoint Server project charter?

40. Environmental stewardship and sustainability considerations: what is the process that will be used to ensure compliance with the environmental stewardship policy?

1.2 Stakeholder Register: Microsoft SharePoint Server

41. Who wants to talk about Security?

42. Who is managing stakeholder engagement?

43. How will reports be created?

44. What & Why?

45. What is the power of the stakeholder?

46. What are the major Microsoft SharePoint Server project milestones requiring communications or providing communications opportunities?

47. How should employers make voices heard?

48. How much influence do they have on the Microsoft SharePoint Server project?

49. What opportunities exist to provide communications?

50. Is your organization ready for change?

51. How big is the gap?

1.3 Stakeholder Analysis Matrix: Microsoft SharePoint Server

52. Has there been a similar initiative in the region?

53. Alliances: with which other actors is the actor allied, how are they interconnected?

54. Why do you care?

55. Are you working on the right risks?

56. What are the key services, contractual arrangements, or other relationships between stakeholder groups?

57. How affected by the problem(s)?

58. Who has been involved in the area (thematic or geographic) in the past?

59. Competitive advantages?

60. Partnership opportunities/synergies?

61. Identify the stakeholders levels most frequently used –or at least sought– in your Microsoft SharePoint Server projects and for which purpose?

62. What obstacles does your organization face?

63. How much do resources cost?

64. Who is most interested in information about the topic and/or has previously initiated interest?

65. Innovative aspects?

66. What is accountability in relation to the Microsoft SharePoint Server project?

67. Contributions to policy and practice?

68. What are the mechanisms of public and social accountability, and how can they be made better?

69. Who has control over whom?

70. Seasonality, weather effects?

71. Business and product development?

2.0 Planning Process Group: Microsoft SharePoint Server

72. In what way has the Microsoft SharePoint Server project come up with innovative measures for problem-solving?

73. How many days can task X be late in starting without affecting the Microsoft SharePoint Server project completion date?

74. To what extent has the intervention strategy been adapted to the areas of intervention in which it is being implemented?

75. The Microsoft SharePoint Server project charter is created in which Microsoft SharePoint Server project management process group?

76. Does the program have follow-up mechanisms (to verify the quality of the products, punctuality of delivery, etc.) to measure progress in the achievement of the envisaged results?

77. How will it affect you?

78. Do the partners have sufficient financial capacity to keep up the benefits produced by the programme?

79. What makes your Microsoft SharePoint Server project successful?

80. Why do it Microsoft SharePoint Server projects

fail?

81. Professionals want to know what is expected from them; what are the deliverables?

82. To what extent and in what ways are the Microsoft SharePoint Server project contributing to progress towards organizational reform?

83. To what extent is the program helping to influence your organizations policy framework?

84. To what extent have the target population and participants made the activities own, taking an active role in it?

85. Is the Microsoft SharePoint Server project supported by national and/or local organizations?

86. What is the difference between the early schedule and late schedule?

87. Will the products created live up to the necessary quality?

88. In what way has the program contributed towards the issue culture and development included on the public agenda?

89. How does activity resource estimation affect activity duration estimation?

90. To what extent do the intervention objectives and strategies of the Microsoft SharePoint Server project respond to your organizations plans?

2.1 Project Management Plan: Microsoft SharePoint Server

91. What would you do differently what did not work?

92. Does the implementation plan have an appropriate division of responsibilities?

93. Do the proposed changes from the Microsoft SharePoint Server project include any significant risks to safety?

94. What data/reports/tools/etc. do your PMs need?

95. What did not work so well?

96. Are there non-structural buyout or relocation recommendations?

97. Are comparable cost estimates used for comparing, screening and selecting alternative plans, and has a reasonable cost estimate been developed for the recommended plan?

98. What is risk management?

99. How do you manage time?

100. What should you drop in order to add something new?

101. Who is the Microsoft SharePoint Server project Manager?

102. What is the justification?

103. Is the budget realistic?

104. Has the selected plan been formulated using cost effectiveness and incremental analysis techniques?

105. Will you add a schedule and diagram?

106. When is the Microsoft SharePoint Server project management plan created?

107. Why Change?

108. Are alternatives safe, functional, constructible, economical, reasonable and sustainable?

2.2 Scope Management Plan: Microsoft SharePoint Server

109. Has the Microsoft SharePoint Server project manager been identified?

110. Are the existing and future without-plan conditions reasonable and appropriate?

111. Why is a scope management plan important?

112. What threats might prevent you from getting there?

113. What is the need the Microsoft SharePoint Server project will address?

114. Does the title convey to the reader the essence of the Microsoft SharePoint Server project?

115. Deliverables -are the deliverables tangible and verifiable?

116. How are you planning to maintain the scope baseline and how will you manage scope changes?

117. Is there a requirements change management processes in place?

118. Are action items captured and managed?

119. What strengths do you have?

120. What does the critical path really mean?

121. What are the risks that could significantly affect the resources needed for the Microsoft SharePoint Server project?

122. Has a capability assessment been conducted?

123. Why do you need to manage scope?

124. Is there an approved case?

125. Organizational policies that might affect the availability of resources?

126. Do all stakeholders know how to access this repository and where to find the Microsoft SharePoint Server project documentation?

127. Is each item clearly and completely defined?

128. Are the payment terms being followed?

2.3 Requirements Management Plan: Microsoft SharePoint Server

129. Will the Microsoft SharePoint Server project requirements become approved in writing?

130. Will you use tracing to help understand the impact of a change in requirements?

131. What are you trying to do?

132. Who will initially review the Microsoft SharePoint Server project work or products to ensure it meets the applicable acceptance criteria?

133. Is any organizational data being used or stored?

134. Who will approve the requirements (and if multiple approvers, in what order)?

135. Do you really need to write this document at all?

136. In case of software development; Should you have a test for each code module?

137. Will the contractors involved take full responsibility?

138. Do you know which stakeholders will participate in the requirements effort?

139. Subject to change control?

140. What performance metrics will be used?

141. What information regarding the Microsoft SharePoint Server project requirements will be reported?

142. Is the user satisfied?

143. Will you perform a Requirements Risk assessment and develop a plan to deal with risks?

144. Is the change control process documented?

145. Controlling Microsoft SharePoint Server project requirements involves monitoring the status of the Microsoft SharePoint Server project requirements and managing changes to the requirements. Who is responsible for monitoring and tracking the Microsoft SharePoint Server project requirements?

146. Could inaccurate or incomplete requirements in this Microsoft SharePoint Server project create a serious risk for the business?

147. Is the system software (non-operating system) new to the IT Microsoft SharePoint Server project team?

148. Have stakeholders been instructed in the Change Control process?

2.4 Requirements Documentation: Microsoft SharePoint Server

149. What variations exist for a process?

150. What marketing channels do you want to use: e-mail, letter or sms?

151. How to document system requirements?

152. Who is interacting with the system?

153. Where are business rules being captured?

154. Does your organization restrict technical alternatives?

155. How can you document system requirements?

156. Who provides requirements?

157. Are there any requirements conflicts?

158. Are all functions required by the customer included?

159. Where do you define what is a customer, what are the attributes of customer?

160. Completeness. are all functions required by the customer included?

161. How will requirements be documented and who

signs off on them?

162. What are the acceptance criteria?

163. Validity. does the system provide the functions which best support the customers needs?

164. Is the origin of the requirement clearly stated?

165. What can tools do for us?

166. Is the requirement realistically testable?

167. Verifiability. can the requirements be checked?

168. What happens when requirements are wrong?

2.5 Requirements Traceability Matrix: Microsoft SharePoint Server

169. What percentage of Microsoft SharePoint Server projects are producing traceability matrices between requirements and other work products?

170. Is there a requirements traceability process in place?

171. What is the WBS?

172. What are the chronologies, contingencies, consequences, criteria?

173. Describe the process for approving requirements so they can be added to the traceability matrix and Microsoft SharePoint Server project work can be performed. Will the Microsoft SharePoint Server project requirements become approved in writing?

174. Do you have a clear understanding of all subcontracts in place?

175. Why use a WBS?

176. How will it affect the stakeholders personally in their career?

177. How small is small enough?

178. Why do you manage scope?

179. Will you use a Requirements Traceability Matrix?

180. How do you manage scope?

2.6 Project Scope Statement: Microsoft SharePoint Server

181. Is there a Change Management Board?

182. Is your organization structure appropriate for the Microsoft SharePoint Server projects size and complexity?

183. What went wrong?

184. What is the product of this Microsoft SharePoint Server project?

185. Has everyone approved the Microsoft SharePoint Server projects scope statement?

186. Did your Microsoft SharePoint Server project ask for this?

187. What is change?

188. Will the qa related information be reported regularly as part of the status reporting mechanisms?

189. Will statistics related to QA be collected, trends analyzed, and problems raised as issues?

190. Has the Microsoft SharePoint Server project scope statement been reviewed as part of the baseline process?

191. Write a brief purpose statement for this Microsoft

SharePoint Server project. Include a business justification statement. What is the product of this Microsoft SharePoint Server project?

192. What are the major deliverables of the Microsoft SharePoint Server project?

193. Relevant - ask yourself can you get there; why are you doing this Microsoft SharePoint Server project?

194. Will the risk status be reported to management on a regular and frequent basis?

195. Is the Microsoft SharePoint Server project manager qualified and experienced in Microsoft SharePoint Server project management?

196. Will this process be communicated to the customer and Microsoft SharePoint Server project team?

197. Is an issue management process documented and filed?

198. Do you anticipate new stakeholders joining the Microsoft SharePoint Server project over time?

199. What is a process you might recommend to verify the accuracy of the research deliverable?

2.7 Assumption and Constraint Log: Microsoft SharePoint Server

200. What to do at recovery?

201. What if failure during recovery?

202. Have all involved stakeholders and work groups committed to the Microsoft SharePoint Server project?

203. Is the definition of the Microsoft SharePoint Server project scope clear; what needs to be accomplished?

204. Is this process still needed?

205. Does the document/deliverable meet general requirements (for example, statement of work) for all deliverables?

206. Have adequate resources been provided by management to ensure Microsoft SharePoint Server project success?

207. After observing execution of process, is it in compliance with the documented Plan?

208. Do the requirements meet the standards of correctness, completeness, consistency, accuracy, and readability?

209. Have all stakeholders been identified?

210. Have the scope, objectives, costs, benefits and impacts been communicated to all involved and/or impacted stakeholders and work groups?

211. How are new requirements or changes to requirements identified?

212. What is positive about the current process?

213. How many Microsoft SharePoint Server project staff does this specific process affect?

214. Does a documented Microsoft SharePoint Server project organizational policy & plan (i.e. governance model) exist?

215. Can the requirements be traced to the appropriate components of the solution, as well as test scripts?

216. Are there processes in place to ensure internal consistency between the source code components?

217. Can you perform this task or activity in a more effective manner?

218. What do you log?

219. If appropriate, is the deliverable content consistent with current Microsoft SharePoint Server project documents and in compliance with the Document Management Plan?

2.8 Work Breakdown Structure: Microsoft SharePoint Server

220. What is the probability that the Microsoft SharePoint Server project duration will exceed xx weeks?

221. How many levels?

222. Is the work breakdown structure (wbs) defined and is the scope of the Microsoft SharePoint Server project clear with assigned deliverable owners?

223. Who has to do it?

224. When does it have to be done?

225. Why would you develop a Work Breakdown Structure?

226. How big is a work-package?

227. How much detail?

228. Is it a change in scope?

229. When would you develop a Work Breakdown Structure?

230. Can you make it?

231. Is it still viable?

232. When do you stop?

233. Where does it take place?

234. What has to be done?

235. Do you need another level?

236. How will you and your Microsoft SharePoint Server project team define the Microsoft SharePoint Server projects scope and work breakdown structure?

237. Why is it useful?

238. How far down?

239. What is the probability of completing the Microsoft SharePoint Server project in less that xx days?

2.9 WBS Dictionary: Microsoft SharePoint Server

240. Are overhead budgets and costs being handled according to the disclosure statement when applicable, or otherwise properly classified (for example, engineering overhead, IR&D)?

241. Does the contractors system provide unit or lot costs when applicable?

242. Appropriate work authorization documents which subdivide the contractual effort and responsibilities, within functional organizations?

243. Is data disseminated to the contractors management timely, accurate, and usable?

244. Are procedures established to prevent changes to the contract budget base other than the already stated authorized by contractual action?

245. Are work packages assigned to performing organizations?

246. Is all budget available as management reserve identified and excluded from the performance measurement baseline?

247. Do work packages consist of discrete tasks which are adequately described?

248. Budgets assigned to major functional

organizations?

249. Performance to date and material commitment?

250. Are procedures in existence that control replanning of unopened work packages, and are corresponding procedures adhered to?

251. Are authorized changes being incorporated in a timely manner?

252. Are estimates developed by Microsoft SharePoint Server project personnel coordinated with the already stated responsible for overall management to determine whether required resources will be available according to revised planning?

253. Are direct or indirect cost adjustments being accomplished according to accounting procedures acceptable to us?

254. Do work packages reflect the actual way in which the work will be done and are they meaningful products or management-oriented subdivisions of a higher level element of work?

255. Budgets assigned to control accounts?

256. Is cost and schedule performance measurement done in a consistent, systematic manner?

257. What size should a work package be?

258. Contractor financial periods; for example, annual?

2.10 Schedule Management Plan: Microsoft SharePoint Server

259. Are adequate resources provided for the quality assurance function?

260. Are there checklists created to determine if all quality processes are followed?

261. Were Microsoft SharePoint Server project team members involved in detailed estimating and scheduling?

262. Are the predecessor and successor relationships accurate?

263. Are the processes for status updates and maintenance defined?

264. Is a process defined for baseline approval and control?

265. Have all involved Microsoft SharePoint Server project stakeholders and work groups committed to the Microsoft SharePoint Server project?

266. Are the appropriate IT resources adequate to meet planned commitments?

267. Who is responsible for estimating the activity resources?

268. Is there a formal set of procedures supporting

Issues Management?

269. Are the results of quality assurance reviews provided to affected groups & individuals?

270. Is the quality assurance team identified?

271. Does the time Microsoft SharePoint Server projection include an amount for contingencies (time reserves)?

272. Has a provision been made to reassess Microsoft SharePoint Server project risks at various Microsoft SharePoint Server project stages?

273. Does the resource management plan include a personnel development plan?

274. Has the schedule been baselined?

275. What will be the final cost of the Microsoft SharePoint Server project if status quo is maintained?

276. Does the Microsoft SharePoint Server project have a formal Microsoft SharePoint Server project Charter?

277. Is it standard practice to formally commit stakeholders to the Microsoft SharePoint Server project via agreements?

2.11 Activity List: Microsoft SharePoint Server

278. What will be performed?

279. How difficult will it be to do specific activities on this Microsoft SharePoint Server project?

280. What is the probability the Microsoft SharePoint Server project can be completed in xx weeks?

281. In what sequence?

282. Is infrastructure setup part of your Microsoft SharePoint Server project?

283. The wbs is developed as part of a joint planning session. and how do you know that youhave done this right?

284. How should ongoing costs be monitored to try to keep the Microsoft SharePoint Server project within budget?

285. Can you determine the activity that must finish, before this activity can start?

286. What went right?

287. What is the total time required to complete the Microsoft SharePoint Server project if no delays occur?

288. For other activities, how much delay can be tolerated?

289. Who will perform the work?

290. What did not go as well?

291. Are the required resources available or need to be acquired?

292. When will the work be performed?

293. How much slack is available in the Microsoft SharePoint Server project?

294. When do the individual activities need to start and finish?

295. Should you include sub-activities?

296. What is your organizations history in doing similar activities?

2.12 Activity Attributes: Microsoft SharePoint Server

297. How difficult will it be to complete specific activities on this Microsoft SharePoint Server project?

298. How else could the items be grouped?

299. How many resources do you need to complete the work scope within a limit of X number of days?

300. Which method produces the more accurate cost assignment?

301. How many days do you need to complete the work scope with a limit of X number of resources?

302. Do you feel very comfortable with your prediction?

303. What is missing?

304. Activity: what is In the Bag?

305. Are the required resources available?

306. Activity: fair or not fair?

307. Can more resources be added?

308. What is the general pattern here?

309. What activity do you think you should spend the

most time on?

310. Is there anything planned that does not need to be here?

311. Is there a trend during the year?

312. Resource is assigned to?

313. How difficult will it be to do specific activities on this Microsoft SharePoint Server project?

314. Resources to accomplish the work?

2.13 Milestone List: Microsoft SharePoint Server

315. Calculate how long can activity be delayed?

316. How difficult will it be to do specific activities on this Microsoft SharePoint Server project?

317. Legislative effects?

318. What background experience, skills, and strengths does the team bring to your organization?

319. Marketing - reach, distribution, awareness?

320. Global influences?

321. Political effects?

322. How late can the activity start?

323. Identify critical paths (one or more) and which activities are on the critical path?

324. Can you derive how soon can the whole Microsoft SharePoint Server project finish?

325. Continuity, supply chain robustness?

326. What would happen if a delivery of material was one week late?

327. Environmental effects?

328. Insurmountable weaknesses?

329. Level of the Innovation?

330. How will the milestone be verified?

331. Which path is the critical path?

332. Vital contracts and partners?

2.14 Network Diagram: Microsoft SharePoint Server

333. What controls the start and finish of a job?

334. What is the completion time?

335. What can be done concurrently?

336. What are the Major Administrative Issues?

337. If a current contract exists, can you provide the vendor name, contract start, and contract expiration date?

338. What are the Key Success Factors?

339. What is the lowest cost to complete this Microsoft SharePoint Server project in xx weeks?

340. If the Microsoft SharePoint Server project network diagram cannot change and you have extra personnel resources, what is the BEST thing to do?

341. How difficult will it be to do specific activities on this Microsoft SharePoint Server project?

342. What job or jobs precede it?

343. Where do you schedule uncertainty time?

344. What to do and When?

345. What are the tools?

346. What job or jobs follow it?

347. What activities must occur simultaneously with this activity?

348. How confident can you be in your milestone dates and the delivery date?

349. Why must you schedule milestones, such as reviews, throughout the Microsoft SharePoint Server project?

350. Are you on time?

351. What is the probability of completing the Microsoft SharePoint Server project in less that xx days?

352. Which type of network diagram allows you to depict four types of dependencies?

2.15 Activity Resource Requirements: Microsoft SharePoint Server

353. What are constraints that you might find during the Human Resource Planning process?

354. Do you use tools like decomposition and rolling-wave planning to produce the activity list and other outputs?

355. When does monitoring begin?

356. Time for overtime?

357. How do you handle petty cash?

358. How many signatures do you require on a check and does this match what is in your policy and procedures?

359. Organizational Applicability?

360. Are there unresolved issues that need to be addressed?

361. What is the Work Plan Standard?

362. Anything else?

363. Other support in specific areas?

364. Which logical relationship does the PDM use most often?

365. Why do you do that?

2.16 Resource Breakdown Structure: Microsoft SharePoint Server

366. Who is allowed to see what data about which resources?

367. What are the requirements for resource data?

368. Why time management?

369. How should the information be delivered?

370. Who needs what information?

371. Is predictive resource analysis being done?

372. Why is this important?

373. The list could probably go on, but, the thing that you would most like to know is, How long & How much?

374. How difficult will it be to do specific activities on this Microsoft SharePoint Server project?

375. Who will be used as a Microsoft SharePoint Server project team member?

376. What is Microsoft SharePoint Server project communication management?

377. Why do you do it?

378. Any changes from stakeholders?

379. Which resources should be in the resource pool?

380. When do they need the information?

381. Goals for the Microsoft SharePoint Server project. What is each stakeholders desired outcome for the Microsoft SharePoint Server project?

382. Which resource planning tool provides information on resource responsibility and accountability?

2.17 Activity Duration Estimates: Microsoft SharePoint Server

383. How does a Microsoft SharePoint Server project life cycle differ from a product life cycle?

384. How do functionality, system outputs, performance, reliability, and maintainability requirements affect quality planning?

385. Do your results resemble a normal distribution?

386. Which is a benefit of an analogous Microsoft SharePoint Server project estimate?

387. Do procedures exist that identify when and how human resources are introduced and removed from the Microsoft SharePoint Server project?

388. Do stakeholders follow a procedure for formally accepting the Microsoft SharePoint Server project scope?

389. Does a procedure exist to ensure the Microsoft SharePoint Server project work is completed in the appropriate sequence and on time?

390. Are training needs identified when resources do not have the required skills to complete Microsoft SharePoint Server project activities?

391. Who has the PRIMARY responsibility to solve this problem?

392. Where do schedules come from?

393. Is a contract change control system defined to manage changes to contract terms and conditions?

394. Are Microsoft SharePoint Server project records organized, maintained, and assessable by Microsoft SharePoint Server project team members?

395. Which frame seemed to be the most important and why?

396. Which best describes how this affects the Microsoft SharePoint Server project?

397. Are updates on work results collected and used as inputs to the performance reporting process?

398. What functions does this software provide that cannot be done easily using other tools such as a spreadsheet or database?

399. What is the difference between % Complete and % work?

400. Which includes asking team members about the time estimates for activities and reaching agreement on the calendar date for each activity?

401. What are two suggestions for ensuring adequate change control on Microsoft SharePoint Server projects that involve outside contracts?

2.18 Duration Estimating Worksheet: Microsoft SharePoint Server

402. Is this operation cost effective?

403. Is the Microsoft SharePoint Server project responsive to community need?

404. What is cost and Microsoft SharePoint Server project cost management?

405. Can the Microsoft SharePoint Server project be constructed as planned?

406. When does your organization expect to be able to complete it?

407. What info is needed?

408. What is next?

409. When, then?

410. Is a construction detail attached (to aid in explanation)?

411. How should ongoing costs be monitored to try to keep the Microsoft SharePoint Server project within budget?

412. What is the total time required to complete the Microsoft SharePoint Server project if no delays occur?

413. Why estimate costs?

414. What is your role?

415. What are the critical bottleneck activities?

416. Why estimate time and cost?

417. Done before proceeding with this activity or what can be done concurrently?

418. Will the Microsoft SharePoint Server project collaborate with the local community and leverage resources?

2.19 Project Schedule: Microsoft SharePoint Server

419. Why do you think schedule issues often cause the most conflicts on Microsoft SharePoint Server projects?

420. Are quality inspections and review activities listed in the Microsoft SharePoint Server project schedule(s)?

421. Meet requirements?

422. To what degree is do you feel the entire team was committed to the Microsoft SharePoint Server project schedule?

423. What is the most mis-scheduled part of process?

424. Why is software Microsoft SharePoint Server project disaster so common?

425. How do you manage Microsoft SharePoint Server project Risk?

426. Activity charts and bar charts are graphical representations of a Microsoft SharePoint Server project schedule ...how do they differ?

427. Is Microsoft SharePoint Server project work proceeding in accordance with the original Microsoft SharePoint Server project schedule?

428. Did the Microsoft SharePoint Server project come in on schedule?

429. Microsoft SharePoint Server project work estimates Who is managing the work estimate quality of work tasks in the Microsoft SharePoint Server project schedule?

430. Does the condition or event threaten the Microsoft SharePoint Server projects objectives in any ways?

431. If you can not fix it, how do you do it differently?

432. How can slack be negative?

433. What documents, if any, will the subcontractor provide (eg Microsoft SharePoint Server project schedule, quality plan etc)?

434. Is infrastructure setup part of your Microsoft SharePoint Server project?

435. Are the original Microsoft SharePoint Server project schedule and budget realistic?

2.20 Cost Management Plan: Microsoft SharePoint Server

436. Are actuals compared against estimates to analyze and correct variances?

437. Has a resource management plan been created?

438. Is the steering committee active in Microsoft SharePoint Server project oversight?

439. Is documentation created for communication with the suppliers and Vendors?

440. Vac -variance at completion, how much over/ under budget do you expect to be?

441. Quality assurance overheads?

442. How do you manage cost?

443. Does the Microsoft SharePoint Server project have a Statement of Work?

444. Contingency rundown curve be used on the Microsoft SharePoint Server project?

445. The definition of the Microsoft SharePoint Server project scope what needs to be accomplished?

446. Has the business need been clearly defined?

447. Is the communication plan being followed?

448. Are software metrics formally captured, analyzed and used as a basis for other Microsoft SharePoint Server project estimates?

449. Are all key components of a Quality Assurance Plan present?

450. Have the key elements of a coherent Microsoft SharePoint Server project management strategy been established?

451. Change types and category – What are the types of changes and what are the techniques to report and control changes?

452. Is a payment system in place with proper reviews and approvals?

453. Weve met your goals?

454. Resources – how will human resources be scheduled during each phase of the Microsoft SharePoint Server project?

2.21 Activity Cost Estimates: Microsoft SharePoint Server

455. What procedures are put in place regarding bidding and cost comparisons, if any?

456. How do you treat administrative costs in the activity inventory?

457. What is Microsoft SharePoint Server project cost management?

458. Does the activity rely on a common set of tools to carry it out?

459. Will you need to provide essential services information about activities?

460. What are the audit requirements?

461. Who & what determines the need for contracted services?

462. Are data needed on characteristics of care?

463. Did the Microsoft SharePoint Server project team have the right skills?

464. How do you allocate indirect costs to activities?

465. Can you change your activities?

466. How and when do you enter into Microsoft

SharePoint Server project Procurement Management?

467. What areas does the group agree are the biggest success on the Microsoft SharePoint Server project?

468. What is the estimators estimating history?

469. How do you do activity recasts?

470. Where can you get activity reports?

471. What is the Microsoft SharePoint Server projects sustainability strategy that will ensure Microsoft SharePoint Server project results will endure or be sustained?

472. What is the activity inventory?

473. What defines a successful Microsoft SharePoint Server project?

474. Are cost subtotals needed?

2.22 Cost Estimating Worksheet: Microsoft SharePoint Server

475. Identify the timeframe necessary to monitor progress and collect data to determine how the selected measure has changed?

476. What happens to any remaining funds not used?

477. Does the Microsoft SharePoint Server project provide innovative ways for stakeholders to overcome obstacles or deliver better outcomes?

478. Who is best positioned to know and assist in identifying corresponding factors?

479. What will others want?

480. Will the Microsoft SharePoint Server project collaborate with the local community and leverage resources?

481. Can a trend be established from historical performance data on the selected measure and are the criteria for using trend analysis or forecasting methods met?

482. Value pocket identification & quantification what are value pockets?

483. Is the Microsoft SharePoint Server project responsive to community need?

484. What is the estimated labor cost today based upon this information?

485. What additional Microsoft SharePoint Server project(s) could be initiated as a result of this Microsoft SharePoint Server project?

486. How will the results be shared and to whom?

487. Ask: are others positioned to know, are others credible, and will others cooperate?

488. Is it feasible to establish a control group arrangement?

489. What is the purpose of estimating?

490. What can be included?

491. What costs are to be estimated?

2.23 Cost Baseline: Microsoft SharePoint Server

492. Microsoft SharePoint Server project goals -should others be reconsidered?

493. Does a process exist for establishing a cost baseline to measure Microsoft SharePoint Server project performance?

494. What does a good WBS NOT look like?

495. Have all approved changes to the cost baseline been identified and impact on the Microsoft SharePoint Server project documented?

496. Where do changes come from?

497. How accurate do cost estimates need to be?

498. Is the cr within Microsoft SharePoint Server project scope?

499. What is the consequence?

500. Have you identified skills that are missing from your team?

501. Eac -estimate at completion, what is the total job expected to cost?

502. Has the Microsoft SharePoint Server project documentation been archived or otherwise disposed

as described in the Microsoft SharePoint Server project communication plan?

503. Have all approved changes to the schedule baseline been identified and impact on the Microsoft SharePoint Server project documented?

504. Are there contingencies or conditions related to the acceptance?

505. Escalation criteria met?

506. What is it ?

507. Definition of done can be traced back to the definitions of what are you providing to the customer in terms of deliverables?

2.24 Quality Management Plan: Microsoft SharePoint Server

508. Who gets results of work?

509. Have Microsoft SharePoint Server project management standards and procedures been established and documented?

510. Was trending evident between reviews?

511. Has a Microsoft SharePoint Server project Communications Plan been developed?

512. Do the data quality objectives communicate the intended program need?

513. Were the right locations/samples tested for the right parameters?

514. Are qmps good forever?

515. How do you manage quality?

516. How does the material compare to a regulatory threshold?

517. How does your organization use comparative data and information to improve organizational performance?

518. Account for the procedures used to verify the data quality of the data being reviewed?

519. How are training records kept?

520. What field records are generated?

521. What is quality and how will you ensure it?

522. How are changes approved?

523. Who do you send data to?

524. Is the process working, and people are not executing in compliance of the process?

525. How are changes to procedures made?

526. How do your action plans support the strategic objectives?

2.25 Quality Metrics: Microsoft SharePoint Server

527. Was review conducted per standard protocols?

528. Have risk areas been identified?

529. How do you calculate corresponding metrics?

530. Was material distributed on time?

531. How effective are your security tests?

532. Are there already quality metrics available that detect nonlinear embeddings and trends similar to the users perception?

533. Filter visualizations of interest?

534. The metrics–what is being considered?

535. Has trace of defects been initiated?

536. Were quality attributes reported?

537. Has risk analysis been adequately reviewed?

538. What about still open problems?

539. How does one achieve stability?

540. Can you correlate your quality metrics to profitability?

541. What metrics do you measure?

542. What forces exist that would cause them to change?

543. How exactly do you define when differences exist?

544. Is the reporting frequency appropriate?

545. Are quality metrics defined?

546. Which report did you use to create the data you are submitting?

2.26 Process Improvement Plan: Microsoft SharePoint Server

547. What personnel are the sponsors for that initiative?

548. Has a process guide to collect the data been developed?

549. Have storage and access mechanisms and procedures been determined?

550. Have the frequency of collection and the points in the process where measurements will be made been determined?

551. If a process improvement framework is being used, which elements will help the problems and goals listed?

552. Have the supporting tools been developed or acquired?

553. Are you meeting the quality standards?

554. Why do you want to achieve the goal?

555. The motive is determined by asking, Why do you want to achieve this goal?

556. Where are you now?

557. How do you measure?

558. Who should prepare the process improvement action plan?

559. Everyone agrees on what process improvement is, right?

560. What makes people good SPI coaches?

561. Management commitment at all levels?

562. What personnel are the coaches for your initiative?

563. Purpose of goal: the motive is determined by asking, why do you want to achieve this goal?

564. What is the test-cycle concept?

565. What lessons have you learned so far?

2.27 Responsibility Assignment Matrix: Microsoft SharePoint Server

566. How do you manage remotely to staff in other Divisions?

567. How do you assist them to be as productive as possible?

568. Does the contractors system include procedures for measuring the performance of critical subcontractors?

569. Competencies and craftsmanship - what competencies are necessary and what level?

570. Are the bases and rates for allocating costs from each indirect pool consistently applied?

571. Will too many Communicating responsibilities tangle the Microsoft SharePoint Server project in unnecessary communications?

572. Too many is: do all the identified roles need to be routinely informed or only in exceptional circumstances?

573. Authorization to proceed with all authorized work?

574. Is the entire contract planned in time-phased control accounts to the extent practicable?

575. Direct labor dollars and/or hours?

576. Does the contractor use objective results, design reviews, and tests to trace schedule?

577. Changes in the current direct and Microsoft SharePoint Server projected base?

578. Not any rs, as, or cs: if an identified role is only informed, should others be eliminated from the matrix?

579. Are detailed work packages planned as far in advance as practicable?

580. Evaluate the impact of schedule changes, work around, etc?

581. Are there any drawbacks to using a responsibility assignment matrix?

582. Ideas for developing soft skills at your organization?

583. Will too many Signing-off responsibilities delay the completion of the activity/deliverable?

584. The total budget for the contract (including estimates for authorized and unpriced work)?

2.28 Roles and Responsibilities: Microsoft SharePoint Server

585. How well did the Microsoft SharePoint Server project Team understand the expectations of specific roles and responsibilities?

586. Implementation of actions: Who are the responsible units?

587. Who is responsible for implementation activities and where will the functions, roles and responsibilities be defined?

588. What should you do now to prepare yourself for a promotion, increased responsibilities or a different job?

589. What expectations were met?

590. Is there a training program in place for stakeholders covering expectations, roles and responsibilities and any addition knowledge others need to be good stakeholders?

591. What is working well?

592. Does the team have access to and ability to use data analysis tools?

593. What should you do now to ensure that you are exceeding expectations and excelling in your current position?

594. What specific behaviors did you observe?

595. What should you do now to prepare for your career 5+ years from now?

596. Are Microsoft SharePoint Server project team roles and responsibilities identified and documented?

597. Once the responsibilities are defined for the Microsoft SharePoint Server project, have the deliverables, roles and responsibilities been clearly communicated to every participant?

598. Who is involved?

599. Do you take the time to clearly define roles and responsibilities on Microsoft SharePoint Server project tasks?

600. Where are you most strong as a supervisor?

601. Are your policies supportive of a culture of quality data?

602. Are governance roles and responsibilities documented?

603. Attainable / achievable: the goal is attainable; can you actually accomplish the goal?

604. Do the values and practices inherent in the culture of your organization foster or hinder the process?

2.29 Human Resource Management Plan: Microsoft SharePoint Server

605. What communication items need improvement?

606. How does the proposed individual meet each requirement?

607. What talent is needed?

608. Are estimating assumptions and constraints captured?

609. Does all Microsoft SharePoint Server project documentation reside in a common repository for easy access?

610. Identify who is needed on the core Microsoft SharePoint Server project team to complete Microsoft SharePoint Server project deliverables and achieve its goals and objectives. What skills, knowledge and experiences are required?

611. Does the schedule include Microsoft SharePoint Server project management time and change request analysis time?

612. Are multiple estimation methods being employed?

613. Have the key functions and capabilities been defined and assigned to each release or iteration?

614. What skills, knowledge and experiences are required?

615. Personnel with expertise?

616. Is current scope of the Microsoft SharePoint Server project substantially different than that originally defined?

617. Is it possible to track all classes of Microsoft SharePoint Server project work (e.g. scheduled, un-scheduled, defect repair, etc.)?

618. How will the Microsoft SharePoint Server project manage expectations & meet needs and requirements?

619. How are you going to ensure that you have a well motivated workforce?

620. Are post milestone Microsoft SharePoint Server project reviews (PMPR) conducted with your organization at least once a year?

621. Is there a Steering Committee in place?

622. How are superior performers differentiated from average performers?

623. Is the schedule updated on a periodic basis?

2.30 Communications Management Plan: Microsoft SharePoint Server

624. Are others needed?

625. Timing: when do the effects of the communication take place?

626. How did the term stakeholder originate?

627. Who have you worked with in past, similar initiatives?

628. Which stakeholders are thought leaders, influences, or early adopters?

629. Who is the stakeholder?

630. What steps can you take for a positive relationship?

631. What communications method?

632. Who needs to know and how much?

633. What is the stakeholders level of authority?

634. Do you feel more overwhelmed by stakeholders?

635. Which stakeholders can influence others?

636. Are others part of the communications management plan?

637. Who were proponents/opponents?

638. Where do team members get information?

639. Why is stakeholder engagement important?

640. Why do you manage communications?

641. What are the interrelationships?

642. What approaches do you use?

2.31 Risk Management Plan: Microsoft SharePoint Server

643. Do requirements put excessive performance constraints on the product?

644. What are some questions that should be addressed in a risk management plan?

645. Are certain activities taking a long time to complete?

646. Have customers been involved fully in the definition of requirements?

647. How much risk protection can you afford?

648. What are the chances the event will occur?

649. Prioritized components/features?

650. Is a software Microsoft SharePoint Server project management tool available?

651. Maximize short-term return on investment?

652. How would you suggest monitoring for risk transition indicators?

653. Why do you want risk management?

654. Have top software and customer managers formally committed to support the Microsoft

SharePoint Server project?

655. Technology risk: is the Microsoft SharePoint Server project technically feasible?

656. What is the likelihood?

657. Do you manage the process through use of metrics?

658. Do requirements demand the use of new analysis, design, or testing methods?

659. Is there additional information that would make you more confident about your analysis?

660. Market risk: will the new product be useful to your organization or marketable to others?

661. How will the Microsoft SharePoint Server project know if your organizations risk response actions were effective?

662. Can the Microsoft SharePoint Server project proceed without assuming the risk?

2.32 Risk Register: Microsoft SharePoint Server

663. How often will the Risk Management Plan and Risk Register be formally reviewed, and by whom?

664. Risk probability and impact: how will the probabilities and impacts of risk items be assessed?

665. Market risk -will the new service or product be useful to your organization or marketable to others?

666. What are your key risks/show istoppers and what is being done to manage them?

667. Which key risks have ineffective responses or outstanding improvement actions?

668. Are your objectives at risk?

669. What is the reason for current performance gaps and do the risks and opportunities identified previously account for this?

670. What will be done?

671. Cost/benefit – how much will the proposed mitigations cost and how does this cost compare with the potential cost of the risk event/situation should it occur?

672. Are implemented controls working as others should?

673. Preventative actions - planned actions to reduce the likelihood a risk will occur and/or reduce the seriousness should it occur. What should you do now?

674. What would the impact to the Microsoft SharePoint Server project objectives be should the risk arise?

675. What are the main aims, objectives of the policy, strategy, or service and the intended outcomes?

676. What is the appropriate level of risk management for this Microsoft SharePoint Server project?

677. When is it going to be done?

678. Assume the risk event or situation happens, what would the impact be?

679. User involvement: do you have the right users?

680. Having taken action, how did the responses effect change, and where is the Microsoft SharePoint Server project now?

2.33 Probability and Impact Assessment: Microsoft SharePoint Server

681. When and how will the recent breakthroughs in basic research lead to commercial products?

682. What is the likelihood of a breakthrough?

683. How completely has the customer been identified?

684. Will new information become available during the Microsoft SharePoint Server project?

685. Are there alternative opinions/solutions/ processes you should explore?

686. Are testing tools available and suitable?

687. Costs associated with late delivery or a defective product?

688. Assumptions analysis -what assumptions have you made or been given about your Microsoft SharePoint Server project?

689. Management -what contingency plans do you have if the risk becomes a reality?

690. Which of your Microsoft SharePoint Server projects should be selected when compared with other Microsoft SharePoint Server projects?

691. What are the levels of understanding of the future users of the outcome/results of this Microsoft SharePoint Server project?

692. Monitoring of the overall Microsoft SharePoint Server project status – are there any changes in the Microsoft SharePoint Server project that can effect and cause new possible risks?

693. Which of corresponding risk factors can be avoided altogether?

694. What should be the level of coordination?

695. How solid is the Microsoft SharePoint Server projection of competitive reaction?

696. What are the preparations required for facing difficulties?

697. What risks are necessary to achieve success?

698. What are the tools and techniques used in managing the challenges faced?

699. What are the chances the risk event will occur?

2.34 Probability and Impact Matrix: Microsoft SharePoint Server

700. What would you do differently?

701. Which of your Microsoft SharePoint Server projects should be selected when compared with other Microsoft SharePoint Server projects?

702. How solid are the price-volume Microsoft SharePoint Server projections?

703. Can you handle the investment risk?

704. How is the risk management process used in practice?

705. What are the probable external agencies to act as Microsoft SharePoint Server project manager?

706. How much risk do others need to take?

707. Is the number of people on the Microsoft SharePoint Server project team adequate to do the job?

708. Is the delay in one subMicrosoft SharePoint Server project going to affect another?

709. How to prioritize risks?

710. To what extent is the chosen technology maturing?

711. How well were you able to manage your risk?

712. Are the software tools integrated with each other?

713. Mitigation -how can you avoid the risk?

714. How will economic events and trends likely affect the Microsoft SharePoint Server project?

715. Is the technology to be built new to your organization?

716. What is the probability of the risk occurring?

717. Are there new risks that mitigation strategies might introduce?

718. Is there any sign of biased ranking?

2.35 Risk Data Sheet: Microsoft SharePoint Server

719. What do you know?

720. What if client refuses?

721. Will revised controls lead to tolerable risk levels?

722. Is the data sufficiently specified in terms of the type of failure being analyzed, and its frequency or probability?

723. Are new hazards created?

724. What can you do?

725. What are you trying to achieve (Objectives)?

726. How can hazards be reduced?

727. Who has a vested interest in how you perform as your organization (our stakeholders)?

728. What are you weak at and therefore need to do better?

729. Type of risk identified?

730. What are the main threats to your existence?

731. How can it happen?

732. What is the duration of infection (the length of time the host is infected with the organizm) in a normal healthy human host?

733. What is the chance that it will happen?

734. How reliable is the data source?

735. Whom do you serve (customers)?

736. Risk of what?

737. What actions can be taken to eliminate or remove risk?

738. Has the most cost-effective solution been chosen?

2.36 Procurement Management Plan: Microsoft SharePoint Server

739. Have process improvement efforts been completed before requirements efforts begin?

740. Was an original risk assessment/risk management plan completed?

741. Are the key elements of a Microsoft SharePoint Server project Charter present?

742. Is there a set of procedures to capture, analyze and act on quality metrics?

743. Are meeting objectives identified for each meeting?

744. Are change requests logged and managed?

745. Is there a procurement management plan in place?

746. What is a Microsoft SharePoint Server project Management Plan?

747. Is quality monitored from the perspective of the customers needs and expectations?

748. Are issues raised, assessed, actioned, and resolved in a timely and efficient manner?

749. Is it possible to track all classes of Microsoft

SharePoint Server project work (e.g. scheduled, unscheduled, defect repair, etc.)?

750. Is there a set of procedures defining the scope, procedures, and deliverables defining quality control?

751. Sensitivity analysis?

752. Is Microsoft SharePoint Server project work proceeding in accordance with the original Microsoft SharePoint Server project schedule?

2.37 Source Selection Criteria: Microsoft SharePoint Server

753. With the rapid changes in information technology, will media be readable in five or ten years?

754. What should be considered?

755. What is price analysis and when should it be performed?

756. Can you prevent comparison of proposals?

757. How do you facilitate evaluation against published criteria?

758. Does your documentation identify why the team concurs or differs with reported performance from past performance report (CPARs, questionnaire responses, etc.)?

759. In which phase of the acquisition process cycle does source qualifications reside?

760. How do you consolidate reviews and analysis of evaluators?

761. How do you ensure an integrated assessment of proposals?

762. Who is on the Source Selection Advisory Committee?

763. What past performance information should be requested?

764. How should the solicitation aspects regarding past performance be structured?

765. What documentation is necessary regarding electronic communications?

766. Do you consider all weaknesses, significant weaknesses, and deficiencies?

767. What instructions should be provided regarding oral presentations?

768. Is the contracting office likely to receive more purchase requests for this item or service during the coming year?

769. What information may not be provided?

770. Which contract type places the most risk on the seller?

771. What are the requirements for publicizing a RFP?

772. What information is to be provided and when should it be provided?

2.38 Stakeholder Management Plan: Microsoft SharePoint Server

773. Has a sponsor been identified?

774. What has to be purchased?

775. Are decisions captured in a decisions log?

776. Are mitigation strategies identified?

777. What other teams / processes would be impacted by changes to the current process, and how?

778. Is it standard practice to formally commit stakeholders to the Microsoft SharePoint Server project via agreements?

779. Are the people assigned to the Microsoft SharePoint Server project sufficiently qualified?

780. What preventative action can be taken to reduce the likelihood a risk will be realised?

781. Are all payments made according to the contract(s)?

782. Do Microsoft SharePoint Server project managers participating in the Microsoft SharePoint Server project know the Microsoft SharePoint Server projects true status first hand?

783. Who will perform the review(s)?

784. Were the budget estimates reasonable?

785. Have adequate resources been provided by management to ensure Microsoft SharePoint Server project success?

786. Was the scope definition used in task sequencing?

787. Contradictory information between different documents?

2.39 Change Management Plan: Microsoft SharePoint Server

788. Has the priority for this Microsoft SharePoint Server project been set by the Business Unit Management Team?

789. Is there support for this application(s) and are the details available for distribution?

790. Who will do the training?

791. When developing your communication plan do you address : When should the given message be communicated?

792. What are the specific target groups / audience that will be impacted by this change?

793. What prerequisite knowledge or training is required?

794. Is there an adequate supply of people for the new roles?

795. What do you expect the target audience to do, say, think or feel as a result of this communication?

796. Will you need new processes?

797. Who might be able to help you the most?

798. Is it the same for each of the business units?

799. How do you gain sponsors buy-in to the communication plan?

800. Why is it important?

801. What type of materials/channels will be available to leverage?

802. Is there a software application relevant to this deliverable?

803. How much Microsoft SharePoint Server project management is needed?

804. What are the specific target groups/audiences that will be impacted by this change?

805. What are the needs, priorities and special interests of the audience?

806. Has the training co-ordinator been provided with the training details and put in place the necessary arrangements?

807. Identify the risk and assess the significance and likelihood of it occurring and plan the contingency What risks may occur upfront?

3.0 Executing Process Group: Microsoft SharePoint Server

808. Do schedule issues conflicts?

809. Measurable - are the targets measurable?

810. How do you prevent staff are just doing busywork to pass the time?

811. How well did the chosen processes fit the needs of the Microsoft SharePoint Server project?

812. What is the product of your Microsoft SharePoint Server project?

813. What are the Microsoft SharePoint Server project management deliverables of each process group?

814. How can you use Microsoft Microsoft SharePoint Server project and Excel to assist in Microsoft SharePoint Server project risk management?

815. Based on your Microsoft SharePoint Server project communication management plan, what worked well?

816. Is the Microsoft SharePoint Server project making progress in helping to achieve the set results?

817. Does the case present a realistic scenario?

818. Does the Microsoft SharePoint Server project

team have the right skills?

819. Is activity definition the first process involved in Microsoft SharePoint Server project time management?

820. In what way has the program come up with innovative measures for problem-solving?

821. Is the Microsoft SharePoint Server project performing better or worse than planned?

822. What are the critical steps involved with strategy mapping?

823. Who are the Microsoft SharePoint Server project stakeholders?

824. How well did the chosen processes produce the expected results?

3.1 Team Member Status Report: Microsoft SharePoint Server

825. Is there evidence that staff is taking a more professional approach toward management of your organizations Microsoft SharePoint Server projects?

826. Are your organizations Microsoft SharePoint Server projects more successful over time?

827. What is to be done?

828. The problem with Reward & Recognition Programs is that the truly deserving people all too often get left out. How can you make it practical?

829. Does your organization have the means (staff, money, contract, etc.) to produce or to acquire the product, good, or service?

830. How much risk is involved?

831. How will resource planning be done?

832. Does every department have to have a Microsoft SharePoint Server project Manager on staff?

833. Are the attitudes of staff regarding Microsoft SharePoint Server project work improving?

834. How it is to be done?

835. How can you make it practical?

836. How does this product, good, or service meet the needs of the Microsoft SharePoint Server project and your organization as a whole?

837. What specific interest groups do you have in place?

838. Why is it to be done?

839. Does the product, good, or service already exist within your organization?

840. Are the products of your organizations Microsoft SharePoint Server projects meeting customers objectives?

841. Do you have an Enterprise Microsoft SharePoint Server project Management Office (EPMO)?

842. Will the staff do training or is that done by a third party?

843. When a teams productivity and success depend on collaboration and the efficient flow of information, what generally fails them?

3.2 Change Request: Microsoft SharePoint Server

844. What is the change request log?

845. How does your organization control changes before and after software is released to a customer?

846. How well do experienced software developers predict software change?

847. How does a team identify the discrete elements of a configuration?

848. Should staff call into the helpdesk or go to the website?

849. How to get changes (code) out in a timely manner?

850. Should a more thorough impact analysis be conducted?

851. How are the measures for carrying out the change established?

852. Can static requirements change attributes like the size of the change be used to predict reliability in execution?

853. How is the change documented (format, content, storage)?

854. Who can suggest changes?

855. Who needs to approve change requests?

856. How fast will change requests be approved?

857. What is a Change Request Form?

858. What can be filed?

859. Will the change use memory to the extent that other functions will be not have sufficient memory to operate effectively?

860. What is the function of the change control committee?

861. How many times must the change be modified or presented to the change control board before it is approved?

862. How are changes requested (forms, method of communication)?

3.3 Change Log: Microsoft SharePoint Server

863. Is the change request within Microsoft SharePoint Server project scope?

864. Is the submitted change a new change or a modification of a previously approved change?

865. How does this change affect the timeline of the schedule?

866. How does this relate to the standards developed for specific business processes?

867. Is the requested change request a result of changes in other Microsoft SharePoint Server project(s)?

868. When was the request submitted?

869. Is the change backward compatible without limitations?

870. Who initiated the change request?

871. When was the request approved?

872. Does the suggested change request represent a desired enhancement to the products functionality?

873. Is this a mandatory replacement?

874. How does this change affect scope?

875. Do the described changes impact on the integrity or security of the system?

876. Does the suggested change request seem to represent a necessary enhancement to the product?

877. Is the change request open, closed or pending?

878. Will the Microsoft SharePoint Server project fail if the change request is not executed?

3.4 Decision Log: Microsoft SharePoint Server

879. How do you define success?

880. Does anything need to be adjusted?

881. What is your overall strategy for quality control / quality assurance procedures?

882. What alternatives/risks were considered?

883. Linked to original objective?

884. Adversarial environment. is your opponent open to a non-traditional workflow, or will it likely challenge anything you do?

885. What is the average size of your matters in an applicable measurement?

886. How do you know when you are achieving it?

887. How does an increasing emphasis on cost containment influence the strategies and tactics used?

888. How does the use a Decision Support System influence the strategies/tactics or costs?

889. Do strategies and tactics aimed at less than full control reduce the costs of management or simply shift the cost burden?

890. It becomes critical to track and periodically revisit both operational effectiveness; Are you noticing all that you need to, and are you interpreting what you see effectively?

891. Behaviors; what are guidelines that the team has identified that will assist them with getting the most out of team meetings?

892. What is the line where eDiscovery ends and document review begins?

893. What are the cost implications?

894. Which variables make a critical difference?

895. With whom was the decision shared or considered?

896. Decision-making process; how will the team make decisions?

897. What was the rationale for the decision?

898. How consolidated and comprehensive a story can you tell by capturing currently available incident data in a central location and through a log of key decisions during an incident?

3.5 Quality Audit: Microsoft SharePoint Server

899. Is there a written corporate quality policy?

900. How does your organization know that its relationships with industry and employers are appropriately effective and constructive?

901. How does your organization know that its relationships with the community at large are appropriately effective and constructive?

902. Are all employees made aware of device defects which may occur from the improper performance of specific jobs?

903. It is inappropriate to seek information about the Audit Panels preliminary views including questions like why do you ask that?

904. Have personnel cleanliness and health requirements been established?

905. Are all areas associated with the storage and reconditioning of devices clean, free of rubbish, adequately ventilated and in good repair?

906. How does your organization know that its staff embody the core knowledge, skills and characteristics for which it wishes to be recognized?

907. How does your organization know that its system

for attending to the health and wellbeing of its staff is appropriately effective and constructive?

908. Do the acceptance procedures and specifications include the criteria for acceptance/rejection, define the process to be used, and specify the measuring and test equipment that is to be used?

909. Can your organization demonstrate exactly how and why results were achieved?

910. How does your organization know that its research planning and management systems are appropriately effective and constructive in enabling quality research outcomes?

911. Are all staff empowered and encouraged to contribute to ongoing improvement efforts?

912. What data about organizational performance is routinely collected and reported?

913. Do prior clients have a positive opinion of your organization?

914. How does your organization know that the range and quality of its social and recreational services and facilities are appropriately effective and constructive in meeting the needs of staff?

915. How does your organization know that its security arrangements are appropriately effective and constructive?

916. How does your organization know that its staff support services planning and management systems

are appropriately effective and constructive?

917. How does your organization know that its system for recruiting the best staff possible are appropriately effective and constructive?

918. How does your organization know that its system for supporting staff research capability is appropriately effective and constructive?

3.6 Team Directory: Microsoft SharePoint Server

919. Where should the information be distributed?

920. Who are your stakeholders (customers, sponsors, end users, team members)?

921. Who will talk to the customer?

922. Who is the Sponsor?

923. Do purchase specifications and configurations match requirements?

924. Does a Microsoft SharePoint Server project team directory list all resources assigned to the Microsoft SharePoint Server project?

925. Have you decided when to celebrate the Microsoft SharePoint Server projects completion date?

926. How do unidentified risks impact the outcome of the Microsoft SharePoint Server project?

927. Where will the product be used and/or delivered or built when appropriate?

928. Who are the Team Members?

929. Process decisions: do invoice amounts match accepted work in place?

930. Process decisions: are all start-up, turn over and close out requirements of the contract satisfied?

931. Contract requirements complied with?

932. Decisions: what could be done better to improve the quality of the constructed product?

933. What needs to be communicated?

934. Who should receive information (all stakeholders)?

935. Days from the time the issue is identified?

936. Process decisions: is work progressing on schedule and per contract requirements?

937. When will you produce deliverables?

938. How and in what format should information be presented?

3.7 Team Operating Agreement: Microsoft SharePoint Server

939. Methodologies: how will key team processes be implemented, such as training, research, work deliverable production, review and approval processes, knowledge management, and meeting procedures?

940. Do team members need to frequently communicate as a full group to make timely decisions?

941. Did you determine the technology methods that best match the messages to be communicated?

942. Have you set the goals and objectives of the team?

943. Has the appropriate access to relevant data and analysis capability been granted?

944. Did you delegate tasks such as taking meeting minutes, presenting a topic and soliciting input?

945. Do you solicit member feedback about meetings and what would make them better?

946. Did you recap the meeting purpose, time, and expectations?

947. What administrative supports will be put in place to support the team and the teams supervisor?

948. Do you vary your voice pace, tone and pitch to engage participants and gain involvement?

949. What resources can be provided for the team in terms of equipment, space, time for training, protected time and space for meetings, and travel allowances?

950. To whom do you deliver your services?

951. What is culture?

952. What types of accommodations will be formulated and put in place for sustaining the team?

953. Resource allocation: how will individual team members account for time and expenses, and how will this be allocated in the team budget?

954. What is teaming?

955. What are the safety issues/risks that need to be addressed and/or that the team needs to consider?

956. Do you ask participants to close laptops and place mobile devices on silent on the table while the meeting is in progress?

957. Do you post meeting notes and the recording (if used) and notify participants?

958. What is group supervision?

3.8 Team Performance Assessment: Microsoft SharePoint Server

959. Do you promptly inform members about major developments that may affect them?

960. How do you keep key people outside the group informed about its accomplishments?

961. Individual task proficiency and team process behavior: what is important for team functioning?

962. To what degree will team members, individually and collectively, commit time to help themselves and others learn and develop skills?

963. To what degree does the teams work approach provide opportunity for members to engage in open interaction?

964. To what degree can the team ensure that all members are individually and jointly accountable for the teams purpose, goals, approach, and work-products?

965. What do you think is the most constructive thing that could be done now to resolve considerations and disputes about method variance?

966. To what degree can team members meet frequently enough to accomplish the teams ends?

967. To what degree does the teams work approach

provide opportunity for members to engage in fact-based problem solving?

968. To what degree are the members clear on what they are individually responsible for and what they are jointly responsible for?

969. To what degree will the team ensure that all members equitably share the work essential to the success of the team?

970. What are teams?

971. To what degree do team members feel that the purpose of the team is important, if not exciting?

972. If you are worried about method variance before you collect data, what sort of design elements might you include to reduce or eliminate the threat of method variance?

973. Can familiarity breed backup?

974. What makes opportunities more or less obvious?

975. To what degree are corresponding categories of skills either actually or potentially represented across the membership?

976. Do you give group members authority to make at least some important decisions?

977. When does the medium matter?

978. To what degree do members understand and articulate the same purpose without relying on

ambiguous abstractions?

3.9 Team Member Performance Assessment: Microsoft SharePoint Server

979. What does collaboration look like?

980. What were the challenges that resulted for training and assessment?

981. What happens if a team member disagrees with the Job Expectations?

982. Do the goals support your organizations goals?

983. What are they responsible for?

984. To what degree is the team cognizant of small wins to be celebrated along the way?

985. How do you know that all team members are learning?

986. What stakeholders must be involved in the development and oversight of the performance plan?

987. How often are assessments to be conducted?

988. How is assessment information achieved, stored?

989. Where can team members go for more detailed information on performance measurement and assessment?

990. What is the role of the Reviewer?

991. To what degree do team members understand one anothers roles and skills?

992. How is performance assessment used in making future award decisions including options and extend/ compete decisions?

993. What instructional strategies were developed/ incorporated (e.g., direct instruction, indirect instruction, experiential learning, independent study, interactive instruction)?

994. Does adaptive training work?

995. What is collaboration?

996. Does platform-specific assessment information contribute to training placement or tailoring of instruction (e.g. aptitude-treatment interaction)?

997. What are best practices for delivering and developing training evaluations to maximize the benefits of leveraging emerging technologies?

3.10 Issue Log: Microsoft SharePoint Server

998. Are there common objectives between the team and the stakeholder?

999. Which team member will work with each stakeholder?

1000. What effort will a change need?

1001. What approaches to you feel are the best ones to use?

1002. What is a Stakeholder?

1003. Is access to the Issue Log controlled?

1004. Why multiple evaluators?

1005. What help do you and your team need from the stakeholders?

1006. Do you feel a register helps?

1007. Who is the issue assigned to?

1008. What is the stakeholders political influence?

1009. In your work, how much time is spent on stakeholder identification?

1010. What is a change?

1011. In classifying stakeholders, which approach to do so are you using?

1012. How were past initiatives successful?

1013. Are you constantly rushing from meeting to meeting?

1014. How do you manage human resources?

1015. Why do you manage human resources?

4.0 Monitoring and Controlling Process Group: Microsoft SharePoint Server

1016. How many more potential communications channels were introduced by the discovery of the new stakeholders?

1017. If a risk event occurs, what will you do?

1018. Were decisions made in a timely manner?

1019. Did the Microsoft SharePoint Server project team have enough people to execute the Microsoft SharePoint Server project plan?

1020. How is agile program management done?

1021. What is the expected monetary value of the Microsoft SharePoint Server project?

1022. Is there sufficient time allotted between the general system design and the detailed system design phases?

1023. Did the Microsoft SharePoint Server project team have the right skills?

1024. Are there areas that need improvement?

1025. Use: how will they use the information?

1026. Is there adequate validation on required fields?

1027. Did you implement the program as designed?

1028. How were collaborations developed, and how are they sustained?

1029. Were escalated issues resolved promptly?

1030. How is agile portfolio management done?

4.1 Project Performance Report: Microsoft SharePoint Server

1031. What is the PRS?

1032. To what degree does the teams purpose contain themes that are particularly meaningful and memorable?

1033. To what degree do the structures of the formal organization motivate taskrelevant behavior and facilitate task completion?

1034. To what degree are the goals realistic?

1035. What is the degree to which rules govern information exchange between individuals within your organization?

1036. To what degree does the teams approach to its work allow for modification and improvement over time?

1037. To what degree are fresh input and perspectives systematically caught and added (for example, through information and analysis, new members, and senior sponsors)?

1038. To what degree does the information network communicate information relevant to the task?

1039. To what degree are the tasks requirements reflected in the flow and storage of information?

1040. To what degree are the teams goals and objectives clear, simple, and measurable?

1041. To what degree do the relationships of the informal organization motivate taskrelevant behavior and facilitate task completion?

1042. How is the data used?

1043. To what degree does the teams work approach provide opportunity for members to engage in results-based evaluation?

1044. To what degree can the cognitive capacity of individuals accommodate the flow of information?

1045. To what degree does the task meet individual needs?

4.2 Variance Analysis: Microsoft SharePoint Server

1046. Are there changes in the direct base to which overhead costs are allocated?

1047. The anticipated business volume?

1048. How do you evaluate the impact of schedule changes, work around, et?

1049. Does the accounting system provide a basis for auditing records of direct costs chargeable to the contract?

1050. Are there quarterly budgets with quarterly performance comparisons?

1051. What is the budgeted cost for work scheduled?

1052. How are material, labor, and overhead variances calculated and recorded?

1053. What is the total budget for the Microsoft SharePoint Server project (including estimates for authorized and unpriced work)?

1054. Are the wbs and organizational levels for application of the Microsoft SharePoint Server projected overhead costs identified?

1055. What is the expected future profitability of each customer?

1056. What types of services and expense are shared between business segments?

1057. Who are responsible for overhead performance control of related costs?

1058. Are all budgets assigned to control accounts?

1059. How does the use of a single conversion element (rather than the traditional labor and overhead elements) affect standard costing?

1060. Can the contractor substantiate work package and planning package budgets?

1061. Who are responsible for the establishment of budgets and assignment of resources for overhead performance?

1062. Are procedures for variance analysis documented and consistently applied at the control account level and selected WBS and organizational levels at least monthly as a routine task?

4.3 Earned Value Status: Microsoft SharePoint Server

1063. If earned value management (EVM) is so good in determining the true status of a Microsoft SharePoint Server project and Microsoft SharePoint Server project its completion, why is it that hardly any one uses it in information systems related Microsoft SharePoint Server projects?

1064. Verification is a process of ensuring that the developed system satisfies the stakeholders agreements and specifications; Are you building the product right? What do you haverify?

1065. What is the unit of forecast value?

1066. How much is it going to cost by the finish?

1067. Validation is a process of ensuring that the developed system will actually achieve the stakeholders desired outcomes; Are you building the right product? What do you validate?

1068. How does this compare with other Microsoft SharePoint Server projects?

1069. When is it going to finish?

1070. Earned value can be used in almost any Microsoft SharePoint Server project situation and in almost any Microsoft SharePoint Server project environment. it may be used on large Microsoft

SharePoint Server projects, medium sized Microsoft SharePoint Server projects, tiny Microsoft SharePoint Server projects (in cut-down form), complex and simple Microsoft SharePoint Server projects and in any market sector. some people, of course, know all about earned value, they have used it for years - but perhaps not as effectively as they could have?

1071. Are you hitting your Microsoft SharePoint Server projects targets?

1072. Where is evidence-based earned value in your organization reported?

1073. Where are your problem areas?

4.4 Risk Audit: Microsoft SharePoint Server

1074. From an empirical perspective, does the business risk approach lead to a more effective audit, or simply to increased consulting revenue detrimental to audit rigor?

1075. Does the team have the right mix of skills?

1076. Does your organization communicate regularly and effectively with its members?

1077. Is your organization an exempt employer for payroll tax purposes?

1078. Are all managers or operators of the facility or equipment competent or qualified?

1079. Are you meeting your legal, regulatory and compliance requirements - if not, why not?

1080. To what extent should analytical procedures be utilized in the risk-assessment process?

1081. Do industry specialists and business risk auditors enhance audit reporting accuracy?

1082. Do you have a procedure for dealing with complaints?

1083. Do you have a consistent repeatable process that is actually used?

1084. Do you have an emergency plan?

1085. For this risk .. what do you need to stop doing, start doing and keep doing?

1086. Have you worked with the customer in the past?

1087. Does your board meet regularly and document all decisions and actions?

1088. What impact does prior experience have on decisions made during the risk-assessment process?

1089. How are risk appetites expressed?

1090. The halo effect in business risk audits: can strategic risk assessment bias auditor judgment about accounting details?

1091. Are there any forms the staff is required to sign?

4.5 Contractor Status Report: Microsoft SharePoint Server

1092. If applicable; describe your standard schedule for new software version releases. Are new software version releases included in the standard maintenance plan?

1093. Describe how often regular updates are made to the proposed solution. Are corresponding regular updates included in the standard maintenance plan?

1094. What are the minimum and optimal bandwidth requirements for the proposed soluiton?

1095. How long have you been using the services?

1096. What was the actual budget or estimated cost for your organizations services?

1097. Who can list a Microsoft SharePoint Server project as organization experience, your organization or a previous employee of your organization?

1098. What was the budget or estimated cost for your organizations services?

1099. What was the overall budget or estimated cost?

1100. How is risk transferred?

1101. What process manages the contracts?

1102. Are there contractual transfer concerns?

1103. What was the final actual cost?

1104. What is the average response time for answering a support call?

4.6 Formal Acceptance: Microsoft SharePoint Server

1105. What is the Acceptance Management Process?

1106. What features, practices, and processes proved to be strengths or weaknesses?

1107. Was the Microsoft SharePoint Server project goal achieved?

1108. What function(s) does it fill or meet?

1109. How well did the team follow the methodology?

1110. Who supplies data?

1111. Was the Microsoft SharePoint Server project work done on time, within budget, and according to specification?

1112. Does it do what client said it would?

1113. What can you do better next time?

1114. Do you buy pre-configured systems or build your own configuration?

1115. What lessons were learned about your Microsoft SharePoint Server project management methodology?

1116. Was the client satisfied with the Microsoft

SharePoint Server project results?

1117. Was business value realized?

1118. Does it do what Microsoft SharePoint Server project team said it would?

1119. Who would use it?

1120. Did the Microsoft SharePoint Server project achieve its MOV?

1121. Was the sponsor/customer satisfied?

1122. Is formal acceptance of the Microsoft SharePoint Server project product documented and distributed?

1123. General estimate of the costs and times to complete the Microsoft SharePoint Server project?

1124. Have all comments been addressed?

5.0 Closing Process Group: Microsoft SharePoint Server

1125. What is the amount of funding and what Microsoft SharePoint Server project phases are funded?

1126. What can you do better next time, and what specific actions can you take to improve?

1127. How dependent is the Microsoft SharePoint Server project on other Microsoft SharePoint Server projects or work efforts?

1128. What is the overall risk of the Microsoft SharePoint Server project to your organization?

1129. Were cost budgets met?

1130. When will the Microsoft SharePoint Server project be done?

1131. Did the Microsoft SharePoint Server project management methodology work?

1132. What is the Microsoft SharePoint Server project name and date of completion?

1133. Will the Microsoft SharePoint Server project deliverable(s) replace a current asset or group of assets?

1134. How well did the team follow the chosen

processes?

1135. Are there funding or time constraints?

1136. What could have been improved?

1137. What areas were overlooked on this Microsoft SharePoint Server project?

1138. Just how important is your work to the overall success of the Microsoft SharePoint Server project?

1139. Did the delivered product meet the specified requirements and goals of the Microsoft SharePoint Server project?

1140. How critical is the Microsoft SharePoint Server project success to the success of your organization?

5.1 Procurement Audit: Microsoft SharePoint Server

1141. Where funding is being arranged by borrowings, do corresponding have the necessary approval and legal authority?

1142. Does the procurement function/unit have the ability to negotiate with customers and suppliers?

1143. Was the estimation of contract value in accordance with the criteria fixed in the Directive?

1144. Were no charges billed to interested economic operators or the parties to the system?

1145. Does an appropriately qualified official check the quality of performance against the contract terms?

1146. Are idle funds invested, and is interest distributed to the various activity accounts at least annually?

1147. Do procedures require cash advances to be returned by transferred or terminated employees before they can receive final paychecks?

1148. Are purchase orders pre-numbered?

1149. What are the threats to supplier relations?

1150. Does the individual having check-signing

responsibility review the use of the signature plates?

1151. Is it calculated whether aggregated procurement can be more cost-efficient?

1152. Were there no inconsistencies between the several tender documents?

1153. Is a log maintained over the use of signature plates?

1154. Are the purchase order forms designed for efficient and simple completion?

1155. Are regulations on taxes, fees, duties, excises, tariffs etc. not impeding (international) competition?

1156. Do the employees have the necessary skills and experience to carry out procurements efficiently?

1157. Were the documents received scrutinised for completion and adherence to stated conditions before the tenders were evaluated?

1158. In case of time and material and labour hour contracts, does surveillance give an adequate and reasonable assurance that the contractor is using efficient methods and effective cost controls?

1159. Is the purchasing department responsible for a continual review of marketing trends, particularly on long-term contracts and contracts containing escalation clauses?

1160. Was a formal review of tenders received undertaken?

5.2 Contract Close-Out: Microsoft SharePoint Server

1161. How does it work?

1162. Change in knowledge?

1163. Parties: who is involved?

1164. Have all acceptance criteria been met prior to final payment to contractors?

1165. Have all contract records been included in the Microsoft SharePoint Server project archives?

1166. Has each contract been audited to verify acceptance and delivery?

1167. How is the contracting office notified of the automatic contract close-out?

1168. Change in attitude or behavior?

1169. Have all contracts been completed?

1170. How/when used ?

1171. Why Outsource?

1172. Have all contracts been closed?

1173. What happens to the recipient of services?

1174. Was the contract complete without requiring numerous changes and revisions?

1175. Are the signers the authorized officials?

1176. Change in circumstances?

1177. Was the contract type appropriate?

1178. Was the contract sufficiently clear so as not to result in numerous disputes and misunderstandings?

1179. Parties: Authorized?

1180. What is capture management?

5.3 Project or Phase Close-Out: Microsoft SharePoint Server

1181. What went well?

1182. Does the lesson describe a function that would be done differently the next time?

1183. What is a Risk Management Process?

1184. Planned completion date?

1185. What stakeholder group needs, expectations, and interests are being met by the Microsoft SharePoint Server project?

1186. What is in it for you?

1187. How much influence did the stakeholder have over others?

1188. What were the actual outcomes?

1189. What are they?

1190. Was the user/client satisfied with the end product?

1191. Who controlled the resources for the Microsoft SharePoint Server project?

1192. What was expected from each stakeholder?

1193. Complete yes or no?

1194. What was the preferred delivery mechanism?

1195. Were messages directly related to the release strategy or phases of the Microsoft SharePoint Server project?

1196. What information is each stakeholder group interested in?

1197. What is a Risk?

1198. What were the goals and objectives of the communications strategy for the Microsoft SharePoint Server project?

1199. What is the information level of detail required for each stakeholder?

5.4 Lessons Learned: Microsoft SharePoint Server

1200. How many government and contractor personnel are authorized for the Microsoft SharePoint Server project?

1201. How closely did deliverables match what was defined within the Microsoft SharePoint Server project Scope?

1202. How to write up the lesson identified – how will you document the results of your analysis corresponding that you have an li ready to take the next step in the ll process?

1203. Does the lesson educate others to improve performance?

1204. How efficient and effective were Microsoft SharePoint Server project team meetings?

1205. Whom to share Lessons Learned Information with?

1206. What things mattered the most on this Microsoft SharePoint Server project?

1207. Who had fiscal authority to manage the funding for the Microsoft SharePoint Server project, did that work?

1208. How well was Microsoft SharePoint Server

project status communicated throughout your involvement in the Microsoft SharePoint Server project?

1209. Was sufficient time allocated to review Microsoft SharePoint Server project deliverables?

1210. Was any formal risk assessment carried out at the start of the Microsoft SharePoint Server project, and was this followed up during the Microsoft SharePoint Server project?

1211. How well were expectations met regarding the frequency and content of information that was conveyed to by the Microsoft SharePoint Server project Manager?

1212. How complete and timely were the materials you were provided to decide whether to proceed from one Microsoft SharePoint Server project lifecycle phase to the next?

1213. Is there any way in which you think your development process hampered this Microsoft SharePoint Server project?

1214. How was the Microsoft SharePoint Server project controlled?

1215. How well were Microsoft SharePoint Server project issues communicated throughout your involvement in the Microsoft SharePoint Server project?

1216. How objective was the collection of data?

1217. Were quality procedures built into the Microsoft SharePoint Server project?

1218. How effective was the documentation that you received with the Microsoft SharePoint Server project product/service?

Index

CPSIA information can be obtained
at www.ICGtesting.com
Printed in the USA
LVHW031614091219
639927LV00012B/891/P

9 780655 515258